C000163460

CHIPS FOR BREAKFAST

First published in 2003 by

WOODFIELD PUBLISHING
Bognor Regis, West Sussex, England
www.woodfieldpublishing.com

© Terry O'Reilly, 2004

All rights reserved.
No part of this publication may be reproduced
or transmitted in any form or by any means,
electronic or mechanical, nor may it be stored
in any information storage and retrieval system,
without prior permission from the publisher.

The right of Terry O'Reilly
to be identified as Author of this work
has been asserted in accordance with
the Copyright, Designs and Patents Act 1988

ISBN 1-903953-36-7

Chips for Breakfast

A *Sprog's Induction into
the Royal Air Force 1952-54*

Terry O'Reilly

Woodfield

Some of 'The Irish Flight' – Cardington 1953.

Hutmates – Bridgnorth 1953.

Contents

Inside and outside of an RAF Barrack Hut, 1953.

Introduction

Every Serviceman and Servicewoman, regardless of the length of time served or the prominence of events during the period of service, remember their basic training with great clarity. Some may wish to forget, but most in remembering that time do so with a smile.

Basic military training or 'square bashing' is common to all the Services and has been a rich source of material for comedy writers for stage, film and television. And in viewing these comedy shows, no matter how absurd, those who have served can identify with many of the situations depicted. So, in remembering those days, we can but smile.

Of course, all military training is a serious business, with a serious intent. However, when I enlisted in the Royal Air Force in 1953 I gained a more than slight impression that the Service was still on holiday after the rigors of WWII?

Also, at that time National Service was in full swing, so the 'sausage machine' training organisation that evolved during the recent war was still grinding on. With the paranoia of the Cold War then taking hold, thousands needed to be trained for a new war that fortunately never came.

Although thousands did go through such training, sharing the same experience as myself, I have found little that had been written about those experiences from the RAF point of view. Memoirs abound but in these accounts the experience of training is mostly skipped over. I have, therefore, written this book fully devoted to the experiences of basic and initial trade training.

I remember those first few months in the Service in great detail. Events are remembered with a surprising clarity but, sadly, many names forgotten. Where names have been remembered I have used real names, but for those forgotten I have used substitutes. But whether real or substituted names I do not believe I have brought discredit on anyone mentioned. It is not my intention to show the Service or any individual in a bad light. Well, perhaps with just one exception?

It is not a war story, but an account of the travails, trials and progress of an ordinary recruit, in peacetime – a recruit from the Irish Republic who volunteered to serve in the RAF in 1953, hoping serve for only five years, to learn a technical trade, but was 'conned' into signing on for ten years.

As the vast majority of my fellow servicemen were National Service conscripts they regarded me as a bit of an oddity, a volunteer among the pressed men.

The account is a 'sprogs' view of the RAF ground trades training machine of the 1950s, so truly a worm's eye view of that system! But I dedicate it to the hard working and long-suffering, drill and trade instructors of all the Services. With the mishmash of raw material that still comes their way, they continue to work miracles!

Terry O'Reilly

~ Chapter I ~

Late one August morning in 1989 while I was on duty at RAF West Drayton I was taken into custody and escorted off the station – literally dragged and cast out through the station gates by a mob consisting of my former colleagues and subordinates! Thus ended my thirty-six years of service.

In my final tour of duty in the RAF I was serving as Adjutant to the School of Fighter Control at RAF West Dayton. On my last day of service there were the speeches and presentations, then I was bundled out and placed on an improvised 'chariot' (an armchair on a stores trolley) and thus enthroned I was hauled out through the main gate of RAF West Drayton by the officers and NCOs of the School of Fighter Control and into retirement.

So my forced ejection was not some ignominious end to my career, but the performance of a tradition for a retiring Warrant Officer. At age fifty-five I had come to the end of my career in the Royal Air Force. A career that had come about as the result of a chance meeting a lifetime ago in 1952...

It was in 1952 that I had come to the end of my secondary education. I had been attending the Technical & Vocational School in Coothill, Co Caven, Eire. I did well the final year examinations, passing in all six subjects taken. I had gained what was considered to be a sound education and a range of vocational skills, so had a hopeful future. However, in a rural community the employment prospects were very limited. It had been assumed I would follow my father into the Irish Forestry Service but I was not attracted to that as a career. I did have at that time, a keen interest in things scientific and technical, especially the growing new technology of electronics. Building radio receivers had been a hobby of mine for a number of years. Because of this interest, Mr Coppinger, the Science Master, had suggested that I should apply to join the Irish Air Corps, where I would receive training and could follow a technical career.

I was keen on that idea and was giving the matter some serious thought when I met up with a lad about my own age, named Eric Weir. He was spending a holiday with close neighbours of ours. Eric, it turned out, was on leave from the RAF where he was still in training as a 'Boy Entrant'. When I told him I was thinking about joining the Irish Air Corps he scoffed and suggested that if I wanted to join an air force why not join a real air force. Why not the Royal Air Force?

That had been a germ of an idea of my own. I had learned a lot about the RAF through stories of the war and books that had emerged since the war. But that was history. Although I had an interest in aircraft and knew of the latest types, I knew little or nothing of the now post-war RAF as a Service. The British Armed Forces were not among the options that had been discussed in the career briefs we had at school. But now, with Eric's glowing account of life in the RAF with all its advantages over the Irish Air Corps, I was sold.

Although the Irish Air Corps was a small but elite force, it had only a few WWII aircraft and only three airfields, whereas the RAF had dozens of airfields and hundreds of other units in the British Isles and almost as many overseas. At that time Britain led the world in aviation design so the RAF was equipped with all the latest military jet aircraft.

I saw ahead of me a life of travel and adventure so I cut the RAF recruitment enquiry slip from my 'Eagle' comic, penned in the details required, and sent it off...

An RAF careers information pack soon arrived in the mail but an accompanying letter informed me that I was too old to join as a Boy Entrant or Apprentice. At the ripe old age of seventeen years and nine months my only way into the RAF now was as an adult applicant. I studied the fairly substantial literature I had received.

The main document was a typical Services recruitment "glossy' of the nineteen-fifties, full of pictures of sports activities and smiling faces in sunny places. These recreational activities were very much emphasised but there was also some information on trades and a few pictures too. These pictures were of lads peering into the innards of aircraft engines, or sitting in front of complicated radio equipment, wearing headphones and looking very earnest.

I was very much impressed by the picture of the earnest young man with the headphones. This is what is what I wanted to be, a Wireless Operator. I completed the application form with that entered as my preferred trade and mailed it off.

I spent anxious weeks waiting for a reply and a letter did eventually arrive confirming receipt of my application and stating that I would be called for 'attestation' in due course. Attestation? An unfamiliar word to me, sounded like something to do with the Inquisition?

Being a country lad living in a farming community I knew about attestation of cattle to eradicate bovine TB so assumed the RAF attestation would also be some elimination process. I also assumed that failures in the latter case would be just sent home and not shot like the poor cattle.

My father confirmed that the attestation would be an entry exam involving both medical and ability tests. In spite of my deciding against his recommendation of Forestry as my career, he fully supported my joining the RAF. My mother also supported my joining but saddened by the fact that like most young Irish people at that time, I would have to leave home, and Ireland, to earn a living. My sister had already left home and was training as a nurse in Northern Ireland.

The call eventually came for me to attend 'attestation'. I was to report to the RAF Recruiting Office at No. 64 Clifton Street, Belfast. But not to go there directly but to get off the train at Forkhill railway station, just over the Northern Irish border. There and I would met by an RAF NCO and escorted the rest of the way.

I made the journey and got off the train a Forkhill, as in-structed, as did many other young lads. We stood around aimlessly but soon a man in RAF uniform appeared. Two chevrons of his blue-grey uniform sleeves signified his rank as corporal. He greeted us by bellowing, "RAF RECRUITS?" to which we chorused, "YES" in response. The corporal then bellowed "OK, LINE UP, ANSWER YOUR NAMES WHEN CALLED".

There were about fifteen of us, milling about trying to form a line under the disdainful gaze of the corporal. We eventually did form a wobbly line and the corporal decided it the best he was going to get and preceded to call out names. We answered but some names were repeated a few times, but no reply. Some of us, it seemed, were missing. The corporal then bellowed, "WAIT HERE" and then disappeared into the station office.

We waited for about half an hour chatting among ourselves, speculating as to why we were here and what we were waiting for? Eventually, at the sound of an approaching train the corporal reappeared. As the train pulled in he yelled, "ALL ON THIS TRAIN, TRY AND STAY TOGETHER AND DON'T GET OFF UNTIL I DO".

We boarded the train and I found myself in the same compartment as the corporal. Eight of us in the compartment and we sat in total silence for the whole of the journey. I was able study the corporal, now at close range. He seemed an old chap, at least thirty, which was very old in my young eyes, at now age eighteen. He also wore an impressive row of medal ribbons indicative of long and active service. As it was my intention was to serve only five years for the experience and to learn a trade I did not see myself attaining any great rank or being awarded medals.

After several stops without any movement from the corporal we arrived at large station, it was Belfast. The corporal got off the train; we followed and assembled on the platform with the others. The corporal looked us over and seemed satisfied that he still had the all that had boarded the train at Forkhill. He spoke to two of the group, "You and you, stand here", and pointing down the platform, said, "and face that way". The two chosen men stood shoulder to shoulder and the rest of us were invited to form up behind them. That done the corporal said, "follow me" and we set of in 'crocodile' through the streets of Belfast.

We soon arrived at our destination, the Recruiting Office in Clifton Street. I often wondered why we could not have all come direct to Belfast but that was never was explained.

We were ushered into a waiting room, a bit of squeeze for the fifteen of us, but we managed. Our escorting corporal then left. I never saw him again. After a short wait a chap of undetermined rank invited us, in small groups, into another room. This was a large office and behind a desk was a sergeant. As we came in he stood up and spread his arms in a welcoming gesture and in a very jovial tone, said, "Ah, gentlemen, welcome, welcome, sit down, sit down". It was to be quiet a while before a sergeant would again address me in such civil manner?

The sergeant had us complete some forms and directed us to the building next door, the Army Recruiting Office. This was for medical examination – done first to save further pointless processing should we be found to be medically unfit.

At the Army Office we were shown into a small windowless room, told to fully strip and put on a dressing gown; these were hanging on pegs around the room. These garments were very large, rough and threadbare items and smelled strongly of dry cleaning fluid. The only item of furniture was a low wide wooden bench in the middle of the room. We soon learned the purpose of the bench! Soon an elderly gentleman, in a white coat, came into the room. We assumed him to be a doctor, or hoped so, considering the examination that took place. He asked us to stand on the bench, face him and drop the dressing gowns. We complied immediately but he still snapped, "Come on, hurry up! I haven't got all day."

He proceeded down the line, examining our genitalia, poking and prodding with a wooden tongue depressor. Having completed the line he snapped "turn around!" and when we did so he went down the line giving our rear aspects very close attention. This initial examination we later learned was known as an 'FFI' (Free from Infection) and that he was looking for any visible signs of venereal disease or other conditions.

We were then directed to another room, where a more general medical examination took place, including, weight, height, heart, reflexes etc. Also the test we were expecting, being grabbed by a tender part of the anatomy and invited to cough. The doctor who performed the FFI was also involved in these examinations. I was relieved to see that he was not doing the throat examination.

This ordeal over I was told to go on to next test, sight and hearing. I assumed this would in the room immediately next door. Dignity now gone I didn't care that my dressing gown was wide open as I entered the next room. On entering I discovered it was not an examination room but an office! Behind a desk was a young WRAC! She looked up as I entered the room, not at all surprised or interested in my nakedness. She just inclined her head to the left and said, "Next door, that way". Hastily covering my embarrassment I said, "sorry" and backed out of the door. She just went on with her work as if naked men in her office were a common occurrence! They probably were, considering its location!

When the medical checks were completed I was happy to be informed that I was fit for service and given an envelope to take back to the RAF Recruiting Office. As we were leaving the Army Office the sergeant in Reception spoke to us, saying, "If the raff turn you down come back here, we can take thick un's". "Just look at these gobshites," he added, nodding towards the two young gawky looking soldiers working in the office.

Back at the RAF Recruiting Office we handed over the envelopes we had been given and then we were all heaped together again in waiting room. Soon our names were called and we went into the main office one by one to be given a what was referred to as 'subsistence allowance' to pay for lunch. About two shillings and three pence (12p approx.), as I recall. We were told to be back by 1.25 pm but as it now 1 pm it did not leave a lot of time for lunch. We were also told that there was a small café not far away that served tea and a sandwich for 'one and six' (7.5p).

We found the café was it was very crowded so we did not get served in the time available. We returned to the Recruiting Office on time, hungry, but still the better off by 'two and threepence'.

When we had all reassembled back at the Recruiting Office we were left to our own devices in the waiting room for a short while.

Conversation ensued and the main topic was hunger as none of our group had managed to get lunch in the time allowed. Also discussed were our medical examinations. It seems I was not the only one who had gone through the wrong door and exposed themselves to the young WRAC! Someone suggested that she was talent spotting?

Next we were directed into a room set out with desks and chairs like a school classroom. I realized that this must be the Inquisition bit, the 'attestation'. I noticed that not all of our original group were in the room? A couple, at least, had failed the medical! It was just like 'finals' at school. We were told to be seated but do nothing else until told. We were then given a paper each, told to enter our names and date in the spaces provided. The paper had 'DO NOT OPEN THE PAPER UNTIL TOLD TO DO SO' printed in large letters on the front. The sergeant conducting the test repeated these words, also in very large letters. He also explained the purpose of the test, to determine which RAF trades we were suited for. He then said, "When I say 'START' you will open the papers and start and when I say 'STOP' you will all 'STOP'. "Now 'START'"!

The paper tested basic literacy, numeric and general ability. I was a bit baffled at first as it was not the kind of examination I was used to, or had met before! No straightforward questions testing knowledge? The paper required placing an 'x' in boxes labelled 'a' to 'c' to indicate the solution to the question you thought most appropriate. That type of selection test was almost exclusive to the Services in those days but now in general use and known as psychometric testing. The multiple choice answer type of test paper I would discover were used in most Service examinations and were commonly referred to as 'Vote for Joe' tests. I got on with test and completed just before the sergeant yelled, "STOP". The papers were collected and we were told to wait.

Soon we were called in, a couple at time into the main office. What happened next is what I looked back on as my first experience of the 'hard sell' and little bit of physiological warfare! Three sergeants were sitting behind desks and a corporal at a side desk. As I came into the corporal said, "Name". I gave my name and one of the sergeants said, "Over here, sit down, sit down". It was the jolly sergeant who had welcomed us that morning. He was still in a very jolly mood and I guessed that he had not missed his lunch. And had lunched at an establishment other the café we had been directed to. He had the kind of face that I would recognise as I got older as the kind of face that had seen the bottom of many a glass.

I was invited to sit down. He beamed at me across the desk and said, "Ah, yes, Mr O'Reilly, I see you intend to make the Royal Air Force your career". A bit miffed I replied, "Maybe, but first I only want to serve for just five years". He raised an eyebrow and came back with, "Oh, but your choice of trades all require a minimum engagement of ten years"! I was startled, and thought, "Ten years, that's a life sentence. I would be an old man (twenty-eight) by end of that stint"! There had been certainly no mention of this in the literature I had received?

I said to the sergeant, "No, I can't sign on for more than five years, not right away". The sergeant frowned and said, "Well, in that case you will have to look at other trades, there are trades for five year service". With a sinking feeling I asked what those trades were and he listed, Cook, Driver, Medical Orderly, Gunner, Police and Motorboat Crew. I asked about 'gunner' thinking it might be air gunner. He beamed again but when he explained I realized it was the RAF Regiment that he was speaking of. The RAF Regiment I saw as being soldiers in RAF uniforms. I thought' "If I wanted to join the Army I could go next door".

As the sergeant was trying to explain the merits of the Regiment the corporal close by grinned and muttered something about rock apes out of the corner of his mouth. The sergeant gave him a very black look. However, I gathered from the corporal's remarks that he was inferring that those who joined the RAF Regiment had to be closer than most to their simian ancestors. But the sergeant seemed very keen to sell me on the Regiment. Even suggesting that with my educational qualifications I could gain a Commission. But I was not sold. I had no ambition for the big leap of becoming an officer and he was painting far too rosy a picture. Motorboat Crew seemed the most attractive among my now very limited options.

A friend of my father had served in the Royal Navy and I remembered him once saying that if he were joining up all over again he would join the RAF Motorboat Service. They, he remarked, "Came back to harbour every night to warm dry beds and warm 'birds'". I was attracted by the glamorous image of the RAF Motorboat Service I had gained through comics and boy's magazines. I had read of their 'daring do' in rescuing downed aircrew, in minefields and from under the muzzles of enemy coastal guns. I also knew that motorboat crew was similar to bomber aircrew, involving a range of skills including radio operating and machine gunning. Thoughts of adventure now pushed the desire to learn a useful trade into the background.

I asked the sergeant about Motorboat Crew. He pulled a wry face and informed me that there were vacancies but the service was running down. It may not last five years. But he also informed me that in the event of the trade becoming redundant I would be given preference in re-mustering to a new trade. I changed my trade choice to Motorboat Crew, with Police as second option, and left the third choice open. So having turned down the Regiment because I did not want to be a soldier in RAF uniform I had opted to become a sailor in RAF uniform? The sergeant then said that the matter of trade selection was not final at this stage. I would not be inducted for some weeks yet so I could go home and have a good think about it.

We were given rail warrants for the return home, told we would recalled in due course and then sent on our way. I still had my 'two and threepence.'

It was now late afternoon and I was very hungry. I blew the 'two and threepence' plus a few more pence in the café where I had failed to get lunch. I got very good value. A large plate of double eggs, chips, peas, two thick rounds of bread and butter and a large mug of tea. I then caught my train for home. It was an uneventful journey, but well remembered because of a severe bout of indigestion.

~ Chapter II ~

Back at home I had time on my hands so I returned to school. I had been following an advanced woodwork course and wanted to finish off the furniture items I had been constructing. Mr Coppenger was disappointed to learn that I chosen to join RAF rather than the Irish Air Corps, as he had suggested, but at the same time pleased to hear I had been accepted. However, when I told him I was going for Motorboat Crew he was aghast! He asked why that when my ambition had been to gain technical training?

When I explained about the length of service required to enter the technical trades he was less critical. However, he conceded that it should be a very interesting experience if not best possible choice as a career? He also remarked that having served in the British Forces I might meet with discrimination in some quarters, when looking for work when I completed my engagement.

My father had no such reservations. He saw Motorboat Crew as the best of worlds, a healthy outdoor life and serving in the youngest and most technically advanced of the Services. He said that once I was established RAF I would find other opportunities. He also said that he envied what I was doing. He may have been thinking of his friend's remarks, his ex-RN friend who wished he had joined the RAF Motorboat Service?

My mother was just pleased that I had found an occupation I was happy with. My grandmother, who lived with us, was also pleased but remarked, "Boats? You'll catch your death, Jim and Paddy have terrible rheumatism". Jim and Paddy, my granduncles, were very keen sea fishermen. They owned fishing smack and had spent a lot of time onboard and at sea.

However, my grandmother was grateful that I was joining the RAF and not the army. My grandfather and her brother were lost in WWI. Both had volunteered in 1914 for the war that would be over by Christmas. The war went on but neither of them saw another Christmas.

Weeks passed since my attestation, then two months and I had heard nothing further from the RAF? And in the meantime we had moved home as my father had taken up a new Forestry Service appointment. It was a long distance move, to Co. Clare, in the West of Ireland.

I wrote to the RAF informing them of my change of address and enquiring about the delay in calling me forward. I received a reply saying that changes were taking place in the Service affecting manning levels in some trades. However, they assured me that I would be called for service in the near future.

That 'near future' was nearly two months later and in the meantime I had had been offered an apprenticeship as a radio and electrical engineer with the firm where I purchased my radio components. The engineer, who would be my mentor, was German. I got to know him quiet well through our mutual interest in technical aspects of radio. I, of course, was a total amateur where as he was the complete expert.

His background was a bit mysterious, and how he came to be where he was. He was known by the name of 'Art' but he pronounced his name as 'Euart'. I had heard a story that he had been a German agent who got stranded when the war ended?

I finally received a letter and a rail warrant from the RAF, the letter requesting me to again attend the Recruiting Office in Belfast.

But now with the offer of the apprenticeship and the training I really wanted, I was thinking of changing my mind. However, my father encouraged me to stick with the RAF and strangely, so did Art. A German, the old enemy of Britain, actually thought that my joining the RAF was a good idea? He held the opinion that the old allies who defeated Germany would soon be all on the same side to fight the Bolsheviks.

The fact that I might have to get involved in a war was something I had not given much thought. My thinking was that major wars only happened every twenty years or so and my period of service would be well over by the next one.

~ Chips for Breakfast ~

It was a long way from Ennis. Co. Clare, where I now lived, to Belfast. I broke the journey by staying with relatives in Dublin. While there I spent some time in the company of my uncle Victor who had served in WWI. As an ex-serviceman he enthusiastically supported my joining the RAF.

His own Service career had been very short. Like many others of my family, he had enlisted in 1914 at age seventeen and was wounded less that a year later. He survived that and returned to the trenches to be gassed in 1917, and thus ended his service.

He suffered from the gassing for the rest of his life and still carried a bullet in him from the wounding. He accepted being shot as part of the job but thought that the gas was not really playing the game! He had an admiration for the German troops and said that no soldier would have invented war gas. But like so many of the WWI generation, he suffered without complaint and considered himself lucky to have survived.

The morning of my appointment in Belfast I caught an early train and arrived at the Recruiting Office around midmorning. The waiting room was full and it seemed I was not the only one who had to wait some time to be called. Many in this little gathering had been with me at attestation, now months ago. There were new faces among our number, seemingly here for the first time. Names were soon called and the new faces went off for their medicals.

With them away, the rest of us were told we were here for the enlisting process and would now be 'sworn in'. We were further informed that 'swearing in' would require us to avow allegiance to Her Majesty the Queen so those of us from the Irish Republic should now think carefully. Once 'sworn in' we would be under oath to serve and subject to RAF Law and Queens Regulations. It would be then too late change our minds. It appeared that all those present were from the South and an earnest discussion started on the matter of swearing allegiance to the Queen.

A modicum of Irish patriotism and some mild anti-British feeling emerged. Someone remarked that if you don't actually touch the Bible but just appear to it doesn't count? Another said that it would be an English Bible and that also did not count? These remarks were really in fun but as good Irish Catholics they were thinking of the 'swearing in' as purely of concern between them and God and not as a matter of law.

After that short thinking time we were called into the main office where we signed our enlistment forms. We then assembled in a larger room, the room where we had undergone the attestation. A sergeant told us to be seated. The sergeant then said that an officer would conduct the 'swearing in' and when the officer arrived we would be asked to stand. The sergeant added, "When I say stand try and do that as smartly as you can manage without knocking over the furniture".

There were stacks of Bibles on a side table. The officer arrived and sergeant barked, "STAND". We all stood up and only one chair fell over. The sergeant barked, "SETTLE DOWN". The officer was next to speak and said, "This little ceremony is more tradition than a real requirement. Having signed your enlistment form you are now under contract to serve the term you have agreed to and that is now binding under the Law. However, you will be taking an oath which is also binding in the eyes of God and the Law". The sergeant then asked, "Any non-Catholics". There were just two. The sergeant handed each of us a Bible appropriate to our denomination. The officer then asked us to take the Bible in our right hand and repeat after him the words of the oath.

And thus holding the Bible scuppered any idea of lessening the enormity of the oath of allegiance I felt that the 'swearing in' ceremony was a bit like a wedding service, as indeed we were now married to the Royal Air Force, even if it was for a finite duration.

After the 'swearing in' we were sent back to the waiting room. We were told we would be going to RAF Aldergrove. We would be there a few days before going onto RAF Cardington for 'kitting out' and final trade selection.

When the other group came back from their medicals we were all loaded on a coach and a corporal from the Recruiting Office got on with us. He said that there was a VIP visit going on at Aldergrove so when we arrived to do nothing unless we were told and then do exactly what we were told. The RAF coach we travelled in was very utility in design and construction. The seating very basic and it had no internal panelling. The skeletal interior of the bodywork was all on show. As I boarded and took my seat I was struck with strong smell of petrol, hot oil, and above all, new paint. So new it looked as if it was still wet?

I was to become very familiar with this form of transport, the Bedford thirty-two seater coach. It was a standard vehicle in all three Services. A passenger coach in peacetime but capable of being fitted out to serve as an ambulance in a National emergency.

Bedlam ensued when we reached RAF Aldergrove. On arriving at the main gate the coach just slowed as we were franticly waved through. But we had slowed just enough to allow two RAF policemen to jump on. Although I had never seen the RAF police before I recognized them from my friend Eric's description. They looked ultra smart in white-topped caps, white belts and cross-straps. They also had holstered pistols. It seemed that we had been placed under armed escort.

These were the notorious 'Snowdrops' that Eric had spoken of. Referred to as 'Snowdrops' because of their white caps. It appeared that the Boy Entrants and Apprentices regarded the RAF Police as the Gestapo and referred to them as that, or the 'Feds'. The black shiny peaks of the caps of our escort partly obscured their eyes and gave them a menacing look. They had black and red armbands on which I had half expected to see a swastika but was relieved to see they just bore the letters 'RAFP' (Royal Air Force Police).

The coach travelled only about two hundred yards from the gate when it screeched to a halt and two RAF police started bellowing, "ALL OUT, OUT, OUT" and hustled us off the coach. More police were outside, waving their arms and yelling, "THIS WAY, THIS WAY" herding us into a large hut close by. There were police with big dogs, the dogs leaping and straining on their leashes, barking, and every bit as exited as everyone else seemed to be. I thought, "What a bloody welcome!" We were being treated like POWs.

The hut comprised a large single room with a very shiny brown lino clad floor and a row of beds down each side. This was a standard RAF 'billet' hut. When we were all in, one of the police ordered, "Don't move from here until your told". There was complete silence for a few moments after the RAF policeman left then a outburst of exclamations and expletives and more than one said what I had been thinking, "What a bloody welcome."

We sorted ourselves out and sat down on beds and started chatting. We could not lie down because these beds were only half-length. Someone cracked, "They must have been expecting a right bunch of short-arses. How do we sleep in these?" Another chap stood up, went to end of the bed he had been sitting on, pulled it out to its full length and spread out the mattress, which was in two sections. He then flopped his full length on the bed, spread his arms and exclaimed, "This way…"

Obvious, now that we had been shown! To accommodate folding of the bed the mattress was in two sections or 'biscuits' as they were termed. There was one pillow. Both mattress and pillow were of black and white stripped pattern but no blankets or sheets?

Our conversation stopped as we heard the sound of marching feet and orders being shouted. The marching and shouting got very close and seemed to right outside the hut. We went to the windows on the side the sounds were coming from. At about a dozen yards there was a low hedge and a main road the other side of that.

There seemed to be a parade going on. Lined up at intervals at each of the road were very smart RAF men in well pressed uniforms with bright buttons and badges and white belts. They had rifles with white slings and fixed bayonets. The ones doing the shouting were pacing up and down with a clink, clink, clink sound from all the shiny medals on their chests. Someone in the hut said. "Oh feck, it's a firing squad. They're going to shoot us. The English are very formal about that kind of thing."

That got a loud laugh that brought one of the police back in. He bellowed, "AWAY FROM THE WINDOWS! SIT DOWN!". We sat down and wondered what the hell was making them all so twitchy. Soon, from outside we heard the order, "AA-TENN-SHUNN! PREEEESENT ARMS!"

Curiosity got the better of us and we crowded back to the windows. The smart men lining the road were at rigid attention; rifles at the 'present', and bawlers and shouters had gone silent. A cavalcade of cars came rolling by and in one of the cars, a large open limousine, was, to our total amazement, the Queen and the Duke of Edinburgh!

Her Majesty looked very pretty but had her formal face on, as she would, with all the pomp around her. I only vaguely remember the Duke; all that remains is an impression of a naval uniform with lots of scrambled egg (gold braid) and decorations.

At least we now knew the reason for the high twitch factor, all the hustle and running around like blue arsed flies. We found out later that this event was the Queen's first official visit to Northern Ireland since her Coronation and we had arrived in the middle of it all. We now understood, and could accept, the manner of our 'welcome'.

There was utter silence in the hut as the cavalcade passed by! I thought, "Jaysus, my first day in the RAF and I've seen the Queen! Wait till I write home, my mother will think I'm pulling her leg".

The silence was broken when our wise-cracker spoke up again, "Ah, isn't that nice, she's come specially to welcome us". Someone else spoke up, "She's come to see if she's got her bob's worth", referring to the fact that we had, in effect, 'Taken the Queens Shilling'. Another wit added his piece, "Jayzus, I'll ask her for another 'one-and-six', I'm well worth half-a-crown!" He continued, "She's a good looking bird and married to an auld sailor. She'll be sorry when she sees me in me uniform!"

Outside the bawling shouting started up again and the smart men with rifles marched away and then all went quiet. We in the hut started to get to know each as general chat broke again. The complete surprise of seeing the Queen and Duke and at such close quarters was, of course, the main topic. In 1953 the security situation in Northern Ireland was far from the serious matter it did become. The 'Troubles' then were some years in the future. Nevertheless, in Ireland the safety of the 'Crowned heads of England' could not be guaranteed since Elisabeth I.

Our discussion of the matter concluded that it was rather stupid to have put a bunch of blokes who had come from the Republic that very morning so close to the Queen? The RAF police were right outside and with dogs so I doubted if anyone could gotten out and closer to Her Majesty. However, we had not been searched and the Royal car had passed in plain view and within easy pistol range! But from the tone of our discussion it was clear Her Majesty was at little risk from any of our number. All seemed as pleased as I was by this event. If anything there was condemnation of the authorities for what we saw a security oversight.

However, it appeared that most of us had been vetted. Years later I found out that more had been known about my background than ever I had been asked for. I supposed that this was the reason for the delay in calling us forward after the initial recruitment process.

~ Chapter III ~

As soon as we recovered from the surprise of seeing the Queen, discussion turned to more pressing and urgent needs when someone exclaimed, "C_____*, I'm bursting, where's the lavvy". Others declared their urgent needs and the bloke who knew how the beds extended, provided the answer, " The bog's through there, corridor, turn right" he said, nodding towards the door in opposite end of the hut to which we came in.

How did he know? He came with the rest of us? I asked him and he said, "Went through all this six years ago. Never been in this hut but there're mostly the same". It turned out that he was re-enlisting. His name was Andy and he had already served five years, came out, but decided he was better off in the Service. Now in his mid-twenties he was signing on again.

We had not heard the term 'bog' before used in that context. To we 'kuliches' a bog was where turf (peat) came from. But 'bog' we had now learned was the term used for the toilet facilities or 'Ablutions' as they are referred to in the Service. This was the start of a whole new language we would learn in the coming months.

It was now late afternoon and hunger pangs were setting in. Many of us had not had lunch. Someone remarked on that fact and speculated on whether or not the RAF would feed us. It was Andy who once again answered the question by saying, " There'll be someone around soon, and it's the Royals. When there's a VIP visit like this everything goes up shits creek". Of course Andy was right, soon the door burst open and in came this very young bloke in uniform, an LAC (Leading Aircraftsman).

He started bellowing, "RIGHT, YOU LOT, OFF THOSE PITS AND STAND UP WHEN I AM TALKING TO YOU". "Bloody Hell" I thought, "Can anyone in the RAF speak in normal tones". The LAC continued, "AND YOU WILL ADDRESS ME AS 'STAFF'".

We all stood up except Andy, who retorted, "Bugger off you little twerp, come back and talk like that if ever you get your tapes". The LAC looked shocked but took the hint and left? Andy remarked, "Bloody LAC, jumped up git". Very soon 'tapes' did appear, on the sleeves of a corporal. As he came into the billet he was grinning and shaking his head. He spoke, (in normal tones!).

"You saw young Jimmy off. Serves him right. Just got his LAC props up, works for the SWO (Station Warrant Officer) and thinks he's the SWO." He added, "You will not know this yet but on an RAF station the SWO is God, and there will be no other God but the SWO".

The corporal then introduced himself as Cpl. Brady and informed us that he was the 'NCO IC (non-commissioned officer in charge of) billet'. He added, "And as IC billet I am, unfortunately, in charge of you recruits too, while you are here". He continued, "I also work for the SWO, but don't worry I'm not as fierce as Jimmy".

He then bellowed, "BUT I CAN BE A LOT WORSE IF YOU GIVE ME CAUSE" Then in quieter tones and fiendish grin, he added, SWO is God but I am his Avenging Angle". After that outburst he said in normal tones, "Now we understand each other. Right!" He grinned and then said in enquiring tone, "One of you is a 'rethread?

Andy spoke up, "That's me, corporal, re-enlisting". Cpl Brady said to Andy, "Good, that makes you 'senior man' in the hut and you know all about that. This hut is in good nick and ready for inspection now and it will stay in good nick and ready for inspection all the time you are here. OK". Andy nodded.

Cpl. Brady must have seen war service. He appeared to be in his late thirty's and had a row of medal ribbons and an aircrew AG (Air Gunner) brevet. He continued, "And now I have to do what young Jimmy was supposed to do. Get your bedding and 'mug-n-irons". You'll want some grub, won't you? Now follow me and we'll get that done". "And now, Gawd help us" he said, rolling his eyes skywards, 'I'm going to form you up as a squad and march you. Do your best, we'll try and teach you properly starting tomorrow when you get your uniforms". Uniforms? But he anticipated the question,

"Yes, in the morning we go to stores, see the tailor, and get your number two blues".

We formed up and moved off in a reasonable approximation of marching. As children of the war years we all had some exposure to the military arts. Even in neutral Free State Ireland, during WWII, there was a large standing army and auxiliary forces. One force that was formed was the Local Defence Force (LDF). It was similar to the UK Home Guard. The Home Guard was disbanded but the LDF remained and still exists as a force much the same as the UK Territorial Army. Some of our group had been members of that force. Marching together, for the first time, surprisingly, we stayed in reasonable step and managed to arrive at the bedding store still all together.

Inside the store, behind a counter, were a corporal and our friend Jimmy. The corporal said, "Line up, pick up you're bedding, 'mug-n-irons' and sign. Just name and signature, ignore 'last three' you don't have numbers yet". He issued a warning, "And mind you don't lose or damage any item, you'll pay for em if you do". Then Jimmy piped up, " And no stains" says he, with a leer.

We were issued with four blankets, three grey and one brown but no sheets or pillowcase. We also received a large white china mug and all metal, stainless steel, knife, fork and spoon. Jimmy oversaw our signing, without further remarks.

We ambled back to the hut, as best we could, now laden. Back at our beds Cpl Brady instructed us in the making of a 'bed-pack'. The three grey blankets neatly folded, folds forward and no edges showing and brown blanket folded lengthways and neatly wrapped round the three grey blankets. This resulted in neat bail that was placed at the bed-head on top of the mattress 'biscuits' and the whole lot topped by the pillow. Cpl Brady drew our attention to a notice board on the end wall of the billet.

On it were a number of photographs showing a 'kit layout'. I was happy to note that the 'bed-pack' in the photograph included sheets and a pillowcase. The lack of issue of these here must only to be a temporary depravation. Having made a very neat 'bed-pack' for his demonstration Cpl Brady then tossed it up in the air and said to the owner, "Now you, and the rest of you, try it".

We made a few attempts until Cpl Brady exclaimed, "Ok, Ok, leave it for now, time's wasting but I hope to see better in the morning. This is how your beds will be every morning, BEFORE breakfast. Bed folded, biscuits stacked and 'bed-pack' made up". He then added, smiling, "You can, of course, make up your beds proper to sleep in at night, if you like!" He then said, "Right, now, tea, mess, form up outside with 'mug-n-irons'".

Once outside he instructed us in the correct way to carry our 'mug-n-irons'. All clutched in the left hand and tucked behind our backs, leaving the right arm free to swing, and salute, while marching.

We arrived at the 'Mess' or 'Airmen's Dining Hall' as the sign above the entrance proclaimed. In the entrance way, on a concrete stand, was a large galvanized metal trough full of steaming water. It gurgled and hissed like a steam locomotive ready for the 'off'. Cpl Brady enlightened us as to its purpose, "Wash trough, for 'mug-n-irons'. Wash here, rinse here," he said, indicating the two separate sections. "And mind your hands, its bloody hot" he added. These utensil-washing facilities were a feature of all lower ranks dining halls and they gave out a gurgling and rasping sound that was characteristic of that contraption.

We immediately found ourselves on the end of a long queue. Cpl Brady at this point said, "Well, you are on your own now, see you in the morning at oh-eight-hundred, sharp. And, a word of warning. The Orderly Officer and Orderly Sergeant always to the rounds at tea so if they speak to you say 'sir' to the officer and 'sergeant' to the sergeant. And if anyone else speaks to you and you're not sure of rank, address them as 'staff'. If there're not happy with that they will soon let you know". He then said to Andy, "Now you're in charge" He then went on up the queue. He turned and grinned back at us and said, "Corporals privilege".

The queue moved slowly as there seemed to be a lot of corporals and other 'privileged' persons, such as Fire Crew and Duty Staff. There was in reality, two queues, with we, the underclass, in the larger slower moving one. Soon I actually found myself in the dining hall and within sight of the servery.

A babble of voices, the clink of crockery and clash of cutlery and metal-ware met me. And the smell! That 'cookhouse' smell of mass cooking. I was familiar with smell, having worked in a hotel for a short time.

Other uniformed people were giving us quizzical looks. We found out why when the first of our group reached servery. "Why are you in 'civvies'" demanded a sergeant who was the other side of the servery. "Recruit, sir," answered our fellow recruit. "SERGEANT" bawled the sergeant. "Sergeant, sir" replied our recruit. The sergeant shook his head in resignation.

Because of the Royal visit, civilian attire had been banned for the day. This day the whole Station was in number one dress or 'best blue' to use the more usual term. The untimely arrival of we untidy lot in 'civvies' was as sort of 'administrative error'.

I arrived at the servery and now there was a hustle on. Because of the 'visit' things were running late and we were being hurried along. A row of servers in white aprons were wielding large ladles, impatiently shovelling the food onto plates. In order not to dither I chose the first items on offer, sausage, egg and chips.

Anything would have done. It was a long time since that very early and hurried breakfast at the hotel in Dublin. I was now ready to eat a horse, uncooked and unsalted. Pudding choice was current duff, in big rectangular blocks like small bricks, and thin pale runny custard.

As this was being served there was a crash behind me! One of the recruits had dropped and shattered his mug! A loud cheer went up from the diners and others in the queue. The sergeant behind the servery bellowed, "CLEAR THAT UP, WHOEVER IT WAS".

Now awkwardly laden with a full plate plus dish of pud and clutching my mug-n-irons I desperately looked for a place at the crowded tables. I found a space with some of the other recruits. It was not difficult to spot the recruits. Among all the smart uniforms and glinting brass buttons a group in 'civvies' was as obvious as blown light on a Christmas thee!

The large rectangular dining tables could seat eight. The chairs were of utility design, tubular steel framed with a varnished plywood seat and back. A couple of others in 'best blue' were at the same table. One of these had a single chevron on his sleeves. I recognized the rank as JT (Junior Technician). The JT studied us and asked, "Recruits?" When we answered yes he shook his head and said with a fiendish grin, "You'll be sorreee".

Now seated, I could study my very first RAF meal more closely. The sausages were skinless, straight and geometric in cross-section. They were grey in colour and covered in gravy of the same hue. The fried egg was interesting. The yoke was almost an exact inch in diameter and close to a perfect circle in shape and a deep yellow or near red in colour. It had an all over glaze as if coated in plastic. I head later a rumour that that these eggs were made of plastic but by then I also knew this effect was due to the cooking method. Fry on one side only, at least an hour before needed, and leave to season on the hotplate.

The JT saw my critical examination of the sausages. "Dog turds" he remarked. In spite of a resemblance I was too hungry to be put off. They tasted fine and I enjoyed them and the rest meal. Until I tried the tea!

The tea was self-service from five-gallon, cream coloured urns, mugs filled from a tap, activated by a press-bar. It already had the milk in, and was already sweetened. The tea was pale, over milked and sickly sweet, and I didn't take sugar! I knew that look and taste from the war years - condensed milk! I supposed I would get used to it or do without.

During the meal and as forewarned by Cpl Brady, the Orderly Officer and Orderly Sergeant did appear. Distinguished by their armbands, black with red letters 'OO' and 'OS'. They stopped at most tables asking if there were any complaints. A few tables away the sergeant remonstrated with an airman who had his uniform jacket buttons undone. "Do your buttons up", rapped the sergeant. "A bit tight, sergeant" said the airman. "Then you shouldn't be here then. Miss a few meals or get down the Gym. Or both" replied the sergeant.

When they arrived at the next table where some of the recruits were sitting the officer asked about the 'civvies' but was the sergeant who answered him. "Recruits, sir. Shouldn't have been here today. Bit of a cock-up". They passed my table without question or comment. As it was mostly recruits at this table they, perhaps, they considered we could not yet offer an informed opinion of RAF cooking?

Meal over and hunger satisfied we left the dining hall using the 'mug-n-irons' washing facility for the first time. Cpl Brady was right; the water was bloody hot!

I also discovered that there was a place to dispose of tea dregs, which was most of mine. Seeing this, I decided that whoever designed this apparatus must have known about the awful tea? The lad who had the misfortune with his mug wondered aloud how much the replacement would cost him? Andy gave him the answer by saying, "About 'one-and-six' (7.5 p) in the NAAFI, it's one of their best selling items".

Andy marched us back to the billet, calling the pace. We learned that he had been a corporal MT (Mechanised Transport) mechanic. He hoped to return to that trade and soon have that rank restored, now that he had rejoined.

Once back in the hut there was some discussion of our first experience of RAF cooking. Most expressed satisfaction but most of us were, by that time, very hungry. Andy expressed disappointment, remarking that a special effort is normally made during VIP visits. He remarked, "That was your fairly average 'trough' today".

Next, we decided to practice making up 'bed-packs'. There would be little time for practice that in the morning. I succeeded fairly well on my first attempt and satisfactory on the second go and that was Andy's opinion. However, the chap who had the bed next to me on the right was making a right pigs arse of the job. I decided to help and he managed an acceptable pack after a few more attempts. "Never had to do this at school", he remarked. From that statement I gathered that he had attended boarding school.

His name was David McMahon and in spite of the Irish name he did not sound at all Irish. I remarked on this and he told me had been born in India, Irish father and English mother and had spent a lot of time at boarding school in England. Insofar as I can recall, his father was ex-RAF and now worked for an airline. David hoped to follow in father's footsteps but had failed aircrew selection.

He was now going ahead with enlistment but was considering applying for a commission. I remarked that if he succeeded in that he should not need 'bed-pack' making skills. Officers would have a batman to make their beds but surely not bed-packs? It was we of the lower classes were assumed to be of poor habit and hygiene and needed to ensure airing of our beds by the discipline of the bed-pack. But I discovered that it was a very necessary discipline judging by the state that rooms and beds got into when this system was eventually relaxed.

I noticed that two of our band was not taking much interest in the 'bed-pack' making practice. They were talking together and did not seem at all happy. Were they having regrets at joining this soon? But that was not the case. They were among those who had their medicals and attestation that morning. In talking with them later, it was revealed that they had been rejected.

One was English, named Ron, from Croydon. He had tried to enlist at a London Recruiting Office but had been turned down on medical grounds. Someone at the London Office had hinted that his case was borderline and to try again at another Office. He had tried Belfast as the most distant Office from London, but again he had failed. He was bitterly disappointed as he was heart-set on joining the RAF. His brother was serving and his father and uncles had served during the war.

The other lad was from Dublin and he was also very upset. But he was much more bitter and angry than Ron seemed to be. So angry he was muttering dark threats and even stated, "If the British don't want me I'm going to join the IRA". He also had a fit of Irish patriotism and called the rest of us traitors. He gave me the impression of being a bit simple minded and that a possible reason for his rejection. Both were being sent home the next day but for some unknown reason they had to again attend the Recruiting

Office in Belfast. I could sympathize, especially with Ron. I knew I would have felt very badly about it had I been unsuccessful.

We finished our 'bed-pack' practice, and had made up our beds for the night. We were discussing what to do next when the loudspeaker above the entry door to the hut came to life. It gave forth with the following, "Stand by for broadcast - Stand by for broadcast - Standby for an address by the Station Commander". Following that a measured gentlemanly voice came on, thanking all for the splendid effort and contribution to the success of the visit of Her Majesty the Queen. When he concluded the original voice came back on and said, "End of broadcast" followed by a click and then silence. The station public address or 'tannoy' system, we were to find out, would be a major feature of Service life.

After that broadcast it was Andy who first spoke, "I bet we're not included in that 'thank you', we were one of the 'cock-ups', to be sure". I had to agree; no doubt someone will have to explain the bad timing of our arrival. We heard a vague story that we should have been held at the Recruiting Office and to arrive after the Royal visit. However, that did not happen so we became a security problem.

After the Station Commanders address, conversation turned to what we might do for the rest of the evening. It was getting towards 7 pm, or nineteen-hundred hours, to use the Service parlance that we were quickly learning. Andy suggested a visit to the NAAFI (Navy, Army & Air Force Institute). Others suggested the station cinema, the 'Astra' as RAF cinemas were called. The film showing was 'The Halls of Montezuma' starring Audy Murphy. Our numbers divided into two groups on the matter of how to pass the evening. I joined the NAAFI expedition and we set off that establishment. Andy led us straight to it.

The NAAFI seemed a well-appointed establishment, a canteen that served cakes and tea and a range of cooked food. I was surprised to see the cooked food, which included sausages, eggs, baked beans and chips. I was even more surprised to see people tucking into great plates of the stuff this soon after tea in the Airmen's Dining Hall. But then I noticed that the food was more like home cooking. The sausages looked normal and the eggs looked freshly fried with their eyes closed. There was a well stocked bar with quiet a lot of people in, many still uniform, sitting round talking and drinking. Most were smoking; the fug in the air could be cut with a knife!

It was a warm evening and we all felt like a drink but only Andy had a beer. None of the rest of us had yet acquired the beer habit so settled for glasses of orange squash at sixpence (2.5p) a pint. The squash served via taps from a large transparent tank with rotating paddles and large plastic oranges floating in the contents. It tasted a bit watery but it was cool, and cheap.

The NAAFI staffs were all girls, or women really as most seemed very mature to me. All wore uniforms, of light brown material with purple piping and topped by a maids cap in the same colours with the initials 'NAAFI' embroidered on it.

There was a 'kiosk', a small shop that sold a whole range of items including sweets, cigarettes, writing materials, metal polish etc. I bought a small writing pad with an RAF crest on each sheet and a packet of envelopes, also crested. My mothers parting words were, that I should write as soon as I could. Our butter-fingered mate was able to replace his mug from the kiosk.

Except for Andy, few of us had ever seen TV before, so we went to find the TV room. We found it. It was in pitch darkness and crowded but we managed to find seats. It was a projection set and reception was very poor. The picture was very snowy and faded out completely from time to time. I watched for a short time but the novelty quickly wore off and I left the room. In the same corridor as the TV room I discovered a door with the sign 'Writing Room'. I went in. The room contained a few writing desks, chairs and shelves of books. Also, there were a couple of easy chairs and on a small table on which was a pile of assorted magazines. I decided to write my first letter home on this my very first day in the RAF.

My mother would be very pleased and impressed on reading about my seeing the Queen! I wrote the letter, enveloped up and addressed it but realized I did not have a postage stamp. However, the NAAFI 'kiosk' was able to supply one. The stamp cost two and a half pence (1p), the standard single class letter rate at that time.

There was a mailbox in the NAAFI foyer so I posted my letter on the way out.

There was a large notice board in the foyer with various notices, posters and information sheets. I was surprised to see that largest and most prominent poster was an RAF recruiting advertisement? Why that when most people seeing it were already serving in the RAF? Another poster extolled the merits of having a Post Office savings account. That I was to discover was another pointless piece of advertising as savings in the RAF were compulsory! Junior ranks were required to save a minimum of one shilling (5p) per day and these savings were automatically deducted from our pay! At the bottom of the notice board were typed sheets of paper hanging on clips with little labels above them, PSI MINUTES, SROs, UROs, meaningless to me at that point.

At 10 pm the NAAFI closed so we had to leave and go back to the hut. Also we had been told it was 'lights out' at 11 pm. Back in the hut we were still sitting around chatting as that hour approached. At a few minutes before 11 pm Cpl Brady popped in, it appeared he had his own private room or 'bunk' at the end of the hut. Another corporal's privilege! He said, "Right, when I said oh-eight-hundred in the morning for inspection, that is <u>after</u> breakfast. Reveille is at oh-six-thirty, breakfast at oh-seven-hundred. OK, good night". He then switched off the lights and left us in darkness.

None of us had nightwear as we had been instructed not to bring additional clothing of any kind. We were to bring only toilet things. I climbed into bed in just a singlet and without sheets the blankets felt very rough against bare skin. But not to worry, the lack of sheets and pyjamas was only temporary. Chatter and joke telling continued in the dark and the subject of 'reveille' was mentioned. Someone asked how we would know? Someone made a bugle sound. From another, "You'll know. The bloody tannoy will soon let us know!" It was Andy's voice with that information. The chatter died away and I have soon asleep. It had been a very long and eventful day, which left an indelible impression in my mind. •

~ Chapter IV ~

I woke early the next morning, before the tannoyed 'reveille'. I could hear the sound of powerful aero engines revving up, reminding me of where I was, and my new situation. My watch showed it to be just after 6 am. My father had given me an old but fully serviceable pocket watch before leaving home. I got out of bed, slipped on my trousers and made for the ablutions with my toilet things.

Some others were already there, but not from my hut. I then realized that the ablutions were shared by a number of huts, three others, in fact, forming a standard 'H' block configuration. Four huts forming the uprights of the letter 'H' and the horizontal bar formed by the ablutions and services block. Each hut housed twenty men, twenty-one including the corporal's bunk.

As there were only about twenty washbasins in the ablutions I wondered how it would work if all arrived at the same time after 'reveille'. I washed and shaved and was glad I had woken early to avoid the rush. As I finished the tannoy came to life with the following announcement, "Stand by for broadcast - Stand by for broadcast - The time is now oh-six-thirty hours - Oh-six-thirty hours - This is your reveille - This is your reveille" and then clicked off.

When I re-entered the billet after my ablutions some were out of bed and others just stirring. Some sitting up and scratching but still a few blanketed cocoons around the room.

I cupped my hands to my mouth and mimed a bugle call. The only response to that there was a muffled, "F ___* off" from one of the cocoons. I was one of those morning 'hale and hearties', that are never popular in the mornings in a communal living situation.

But soon, all feet were on the floor and a steady stream to and fro between hut and ablutions. I now knew how the limited facilities of the ablutions could cope. No mad rush at reveille but a gradual build up as slumbers came too at different rates. Could the designers of the accommodation have really given that much consideration to human nature in order to keep the facilities to the very minimum needed?

Preparing for bed the night before I had put the contents of my trouser pockets on the bedside locker top. That comprised of my watch, some loose change and a pocket-knife my sister had given me. The knife was a valuable and attractive item. Intended as a letter opener it was made of solid silver, including the blade, the handle shell in mother-of-pearl. That had disappeared in the night and thus I learned an early and valuable lesson about communal living in the Service.

Because not everyone was ready at the same time we ambled off to breakfast in dribs and drabs. I, and the few who had come with me, arrived at the dining hall at just after 7 pm. Quiet a few in at breakfast but a small and fast moving queue. The breakfast menu was very similar to tea the evening before. Sausages, the more standard sort but looked a bit dry and crispy. Fried eggs, of course, glazed with staring yellow eyes. Bacon, rashers steam cooked, pale and foam-covered. Also baked beans and chips. What! Chips for breakfast?

There was also some yellow stuff that looked like lumpy custard. This I discovered was scrambled egg. On the side servery with the tea urns were two large metal bowls of cereal and large aluminium jugs of milk. A dish of sugar was also provided. Sugar and milk was provided separately for the cereals so why had the tea to be already milked and sweetened? I surmised that there must have been a Government surplus of condensed milk to be used up.

By the side servery there was a large eye-level grill thing with a great tray of well done crispy toast on top? I decided to try the scrambled egg as that and toast was my favourite breakfast at home. Heaped on top of a couple of slices of toast reduced the rigidity of the toast. The likeness to custard of the scrambled egg, I learned, was because it had been made from powdered egg. But I found it to my liking and more appetizing that the 'plastic' fried version.

During breakfast some station staff came in. Among them was a Fire Crew who I now recognized from their form of dress. This comprised of green overalls and sleeveless brown leather jerkins. The most telling item of apparel was a wide black webbing belt with a holstered hand-axe. The belt not worn in the dining hall, but hung over the back of a chair. Many of the Fire Crew, I noticed, had chosen the chips? It then dawned on me that these were the night crew coming off duty. What was breakfast for the majority was supper for them. I soon learned that the RAF was a twenty-four service and meal menus reflected this. On most stations on which I was to serve, there would be chips served at breakfast time.

We arrived back at the hut well before 8 am. Some were still struggling to make up their 'bed-packs' and obviously had not been to breakfast. Still, that was their choice, for the moment, anyway.

On the dot of oh-eight-hundred, Cpl Brady appeared. His first words were, "Everyone had a good breakfast". Not getting unanimous affirmation he said, "Well, breakfast is a parade but you will soon learn that when you start your 'square bashing'". He continued, "Right, this floor did not get polished like this all by itself. But just needs a 'bumper' up this morning, I'll show you where the cleaning stuff is". He turned to Andy and said, "This morning I will organize you but tomorrow and the rest of the time you are here you can dish out the 'room jobs'. You know the routine, OK". Andy nodded and the rest of us were getting the message, most of us had heard about Service 'bull'. It would be up to us to keep the billet in the immaculate state in which we found it!

He turned to the two who had not been accepted and said, "Get your things together, bedding, 'mug-n-irons', and come with me when I get this lot organized". He turned to the lads nearest him, "You, you, you and you" he said pointing to the first four and then beckoning them with crooked finger to follow him into the short corridor leading to the hut outer door.

The four returned with brooms and were instructed to sweep all the bed spaces and rest of the floor. He beckoned to two more and they returned with long handled implements with rectangular padded iron weights at the end. Cpl Brady took one and demonstrated its purpose. These were floor polishers, more commonly known as 'bumpers'. Another item that would be a constant feature of our Service lives.

Soon we were all allocated 'room jobs' and I being towards the far end of the room found myself in possession of a mop and the ablutions to clean. Work put in progress; Cpl Brady departed with Ron, the small lad from Dublin and a number of others who had to complete their recruitment processing. As he left he said, "I'll be back to inspect your work and then 'Stores'".

The ablution cleaning wasn't a hard job and there were three of us, one from another hut. We just had to wet mop over the already damp but clean floors and wipe out the washbasins. Just flush and brush the WCs and sink a few 'submarines' that were still lurking about. As we were finishing up someone shouted down the corridor, "Yooh! - Corporal wants you". We bog cleaners returned to the hut. Cpl Brady had returned and inspected as he said he would.

Once completed he remarked "Not bad for beginners but I want better tomorrow. The standard needed at 'basic training' will be miles higher than this". He then informed us of the programme for the day, "First we're going to 'Stores', see the tailor and get your basic kit. As I told you yesterday you will get your number two blue, working blue, and other items. Just the essential items until you get to Cardington. There you will get your 'number ones' and the rest of your kit. Right, fall in outside". We formed up and marched off, almost all in step, this time.

We got a cool reception at the 'Clothing Store' the only friendly face was the tailor, a civilian. The place smelled of a mixture of new cloth, leather and mothballs. The RAF staff seemed to begrudge parting with the kit being issued.

We lined up and progressed along a counter and were issued with, 'kitbags-one, boots-pairs-one, socks-pairs-two, shirts-two, collars-four, neckties-one, berets-one, badge-cap-one, braces-trouser-pairs-one, towels-two, pyjamas-pairs-two, singlets-cellular-three, drawers-cellular-three, knife-fork-spoon-mug'. There was just a very short pause between receiving the items to allow us to state our sizes required for uniform items.

And so it went. The pile in our arms growing as each item was flung at us. We were also given a small coil of thin rope, a drawstring for the kitbag. Someone was foolish enough to ask what this item was for, to receive the reply, "That's to hang yourself if you find that joining up is a mistake!" The tailor ran a tape measure over us, called out the measurements and a uniform jacket and trousers arrived in our faces also by 'air mail'.

This kit issuing process was a cliché in war films I had seen and now I was participating in such a scene! On our receipt of the uniform items someone barked "PUT THEM ON, COME BACK AND SEE THE TAILOR".

I put mine on, jacket sleeve and trouser length fine but I was sure I could have stuffed the full kitbag in the waistbands! The uniform material was of heavy blue serge. I was familiar with the material, as it seemed, at that time; the whole of the working population of the British Isles dressed in 'war surplus'. In fact, my school satchel had been an army surplus respirator haversack. The No. 2 blue, or 'working dress' was officially referred to as Number Two Home Dress. It was of WWII 'battle dress' design except that the choker neck had given way to a lapelled collar.

When I saw the tailor again he 'tut-tutted, and remarked, "Well, a smaller size will be too short in leg and sleeves. Its usual to issue oversize and take in, we can't add bits on, It will do until you get to Cardington, they'll do a proper job on it" for you. I just see you get the best fit and that's the best we can do for a whippet like you"

We had to sign a form as having received these items and were given a copy with the remark, "Don't lose that chit they'll want to see it at Cardington". Cpl Brady chipped in, "Put em in your 'blue' jacket pocket and keep em there". He then barked, "Put all your gear in the kitbag and fall in outside". Our issued kit just about filled the kitbags.

The kitbags were in white canvas with two blue bands towards the centre. When packed they appeared bolster-like and about sixteen inches wide and nearly thirty-two inches long (40 x 80cm approx.). Secured at the open end by lacing the issued cord through a set brass eyelets.

On arrival at the hut, Cpl Brady said we were to take a shower or bath and then dress top to bottom in issued items. We were given fifteen minutes to achieve this. We managed. The baths and showers were taken in a schoolboy uproar. There were two or even three at a time in the showers and the minimum of time taken.

We dressed, finding the most difficult task was managing the separate shirt collars. They were like pieces of board and most of us had to wrestle with these items to get them located on the studs. We all had collar studs as shirts with attached collars were fairly rare then.

Some had made up their ties in 'Windsor' knots, then in fashion. But Andy informed the fashion conscious, "No 'Windsor's', plain knots only". The boots being very new with the leather very stiff, also took some getting on and lacing up.

Cpl Brady reappeared and barked, "STAND BY YOUR BEDS". We all stood up beside our beds but better than that was required. Cpl Brady surveyed the scene with a pained expression and then stated, "You are now in uniform, you're not civvies any more, and you're now 'airmen' in the Royal Air Force. You will now start to learn to do things properly. 'Stand by your beds' means stand at attention at the right side of your bed, toes in line with end of the bed. And at 'attention' I mean like this". He demonstrated by standing ramrod straight, arms by his sides, looking straight ahead. He then ordered, "Now, all of you. STAND BY YOUR BEDS".

We all shuffled into line with some swapping about as some realized they were on the wrong side of the bed. I was one of them. We stood to attention as was demonstrated. Cpl Brady surveyed the scene again and seemed satisfied. Andy who had got it right in the first place was grinning to himself. Cpl Brady said to him, "Never mind, they'll learn".

He then addressed the rest of us, "Right, on all future occasions, if I or any other corporal or anyone in uniform, for that matter, comes in the room, you will leap to attention and stand by your beds, like that. And stay like that until told otherwise. As AC2s

(Aircraftsmen 2nd class) you are outranked by everyone and that includes the station cat. RIGHT".

Having sorted that out he relaxed and became more casual, "Right then, all put your berets on. Like mine. Band straight, badge one inch above left eye, slack pulled down to the right" We having done that he said, "Now, lets have a look at you". He them went down the room inspecting each of us, commenting, adjusting and making suggestions to improve matters. But no matter how some of us tried the new berets behaved as if they had dinner plates inside them. The 'slack' just stood out straight so that some of us looked like sex starved mushrooms that had grown in a strong wind?

Coming to one lad, who had informed him with some concern, "I've got no birds, corporal" referring to the fact the RAF eagle shoulder flashes were missing from his uniform jacket. Cpl Brady said, "Check the pockets". The lad checked the pockets and 'birds' were found. Cpl Brady reassured our naked-sleeved mate that the matter would be to rights at Cardington. Cardington, it seems, would have its work cut out?

When he had completed the inspection he picked the four nearest him saying, "You, you, you and you, follow me" and they went out into the short corridor at the end of the room. The four returned with two trestle tables, Cpl Brady following, bearing a cardboard carton.

The tables were set up and Cpl Brady produced various items from the box including a couple of clothes irons some sheets of scorched linen these latter items I recognized as ironing cloths. We were then given a demonstration on how to iron a uniform. Cpl Brady using one of his own uniforms not wanting to be that helpful to any of us. My mother had already taught me how to iron clothes, saying it would be an essential skill to have in the Services.

Before we were let loose on our 'blues' with hot irons a word of dire warning from Cpl Brady, "Scorch your 'blues' and you will have to sign on for life to pay for a new one". We all managed the task without disaster although the smell of heated new cloth was overpowering. The already scorched ironing cloths did receive new hot iron imprints but fortunately new 'blues' remained pristine but now with creases in the right places.

We donned the newly pressed uniforms and they seemed to meet with Cpl Brady's approval. He confirmed this by saying that he would not now feel too bad when seen marching us around. Following that he said, "Blues now OK, well near enough. But the berets will have to do. They will settle with wear and weather"

One of us asked how he and most of the people we had seen seemed to be wearing berets smaller in the crown and neater than our issue. To which he answered, "You'll find out how but it's not for me to tell you. What's more important now are those manky cap badges". And from the box he produced a tin of metal polish, some cloths and a number of brass plates, which he referred to as 'button sticks'.

He explained, "You will be issued with one of these at Carding-ton which are used like this". He demonstrated its purpose, using his own badge. He slipped the button stick behind the badge via the slot in this implement. He went on, "You can attempt this when you are more expert and until then, if ever, do it this way". He borrowed Andy's beret, removed the badge, applied polish and buffed it with a cloth. He then held up the badge for all of us to see and said, "Near enough but still not good enough, this badge is too new to get a good shine. This is what you need to do".

He took from the box some strips of heavy cardboard and an old newspaper. He spread the newspaper on the table and placed a piece of the cardboard on this and poured some metal polish on the card. He placed the badge face down in the little puddle of polish and began to rub it vigorously back and forward on the card. He said, "Watch carefully, you can polish most of the badge this way but not the crown. Wear that down and you're for the high jump. So keep the crown off the card like I am showing you". Having honed Andy's badge he gave it a final polish with a cloth and passed it round for our individual inspection.

It gleamed! As the last man handed it back to him he said in an enquiring tone, "Good, yes". We all nodded but he said, "Oh no its bloody well not" and showed us the reverse side of the badge and said, "Look, polish, loads of it, not good <u>enough</u>".

He then dipped, once more, into the box and took out a small brass wire bristled suede brush, saying, "You will all need to get one these. They are not issued but having one will save you a lot of grief. The 'Brasso' or dusters aren't issued and you will certainly need those!" He burnished the back of the badge with the suede brush, inspected it and passed it round again and exclaimed, "Now its good but a final warning, DON'T CLEAN BADGES STILL ON THE BERET, the 'Brasso' will leave marks you will never get rid of".

He then exclaimed, "Boots, your boots are clean but still have warts on", referring to the all over pimpled effect of the new leather. He continued, pointing to his own gleaming footwear, "They will need to look like this but even better. Then that's not my problem, 'square bashing' will sort that out. You haven't got your brush set yet and I don't care how you do it but just keep em clean while you are here. Right, lunch time, mug-n-irons, get fell in outside".

As we made to move he barked, "AS YOU WERE". We paused, he continued, "Remember, you are now in uniform so try to look like airmen even if you're not yet by a long chalk. NOW, fall in outside. We scrambled for the door, slipping and sliding all over the place in our newly issued hobnailed boots! "MIND THE FLOOR, YOU BERKS", yelled Cpl. Brady!

Once formed up outside we were inspected again with a lot of attention to trying to get the berets looking more like air force and less like navy. This with limited success but when best was achieved Cpl Brady addressed us, "RIGHT, I know you haven't been drilled yet". And with an evil grin he added, "That happens this afternoon but now you're in uniform do your bloody best to march properly just the few hundred yards to the Mess"

He continued, "Now you have headgear, when you get there you have two options, hang your berets in the cloakroom or keep them with you. I suggest taking them with you, as there might be a few of those shiny new berets missing when we come out. And I don't care how many others you see doing it you DON'T stick em in your epilates. You do that and you're for a bollicking. Roll em flat and stick em in your waistbands.

That said we were marched off towards the mess making a not at all bad job of it with a fairly synchronised crunch-crunch of hobnail shod feet, and more than the usual number stopping together on the command 'HALT'. To a man, we all took our berets into the dining hall, tucked in waistbands as advised. But my waistband was too slack for that so I tucked my beret under my sturdy RAF braces, inside my jacket.

When we arrived back at the hut after lunch, Cpl Brady told us to, "Get sorted, stow your 'irons' but bring the mugs and fall in back outside in five minutes". That giving us barely enough time for a quick visit to the ablutions for those who needed it. But we managed and were all formed up again outside in the very meagre allotted time. However, as the last few arrived, still within the five minutes, Cpl Brady bellowed, "GET A MOVE ON, I SAID FIVE MINUTES".

We marched off and this time away from the domestic site and towards the environs of the airfield. We were brought to a halt alongside a large hanger. Cpl Brady then informed us that we were now to receive the basic drill he had promised us. We fell out to stack our mugs on a buttress plinth by the side of the hanger and then our first proper drill session commenced.

We first learned to size off in three ranks and then proper marching. Starting the march with the left foot and halting without the 'domino' effect that had been the norm up to now. We were marched up and down the length of the hanger learning to keep in step and 'about turn' on the march.

All the while this was in progress various RAF staff would pass by, most ignoring the proceedings. They had seen it all before, I supposed? One or two did call out, "You'll be sorreee". This would attract a withering look and growl from Cpl Brady, which was of little deterrent. It seemed that corporals were not universally held in aw as by us on the very lowest tier of sprogdom.

The drill continued. We learned how to pay 'compliments to officers'. 'Eyes right' and 'eyes left' on the march, how to salute, who

to salute. And just as impotent, it seemed, who not to salute. As Cpl
Brady explained, "You might get a bigger bollicking for saluting an
NCO than for not saluting an officer. And another thing, an NCO
will blame <u>you</u> for being stupid but an officer will blame <u>me</u> for not
instructing you properly". From that latter statement I felt that I had
just learned something very important to survival in the Service.

After more than two hours of drill we were brought to a halt
and Cpl Brady announced, "Now, listen up, the NAAFI van will be
along in a few minutes but you wait your turn until the staff have
been served". That remark was another reminder of our current
status! He went on, "Right, smoke break, but over by the hedge away
from the hanger and vehicles" and led the way towards the place
indicated. In those days non-smokers were uncommon. Very few,
only about four, including myself, in this group, were non-smokers.
The majority and Cpl Brady were soon lit up and wreathed in
smoke.

Soon a small brown coloured van appeared and pulled up
opposite the hanger doors and gave a long toot on its horn. In quick
response a group of people in green overalls and some in 'blues',
most carrying mugs, came out of the hanger and assembled by the
van. This was the NAAFI van. Cpl Brady made straight for it but
saying to the rest of us "Wait here until I call you". When all these
others were served, including Cpl Brady, he called us forward.

We were able to purchase a full mug of tea and a sticky bun for
ninepence (just under 4p) and now knew why we had brought our
mugs. And so, for the very first time, we experienced the famous
NAAFI 'Char and wad'? The tea was weaker than that in the dining
hall and had sugar already in. But on this warm afternoon by now
our throats were very dry from calling out the time to the drill
movements. Any liquid was now very welcome. Cpl Brady had not
brought a mug; he received his tea in a china cup! Another privilege
of rank!

After I had been served I turned around and found myself
looking in through the wide open doors of the hanger. This was my
first sight, close up, of RAF aircraft. To my surprise, and delight,

standing in full view, just inside the hanger door, an aircraft of legend. The wooden wonder, a Mosquito! I had not realized that any were still in service. From all I had recently read of the RAF and from the recruiting literature I thought the jet age was now well established? I could not resist a closer look and went forward.

Two lads were working on an engine. I asked, "Are these still flying". But before either of them could answer a gruff voice behind me said, "Of course it flies and flies bloody well, who are you". I turned towards the voice. Standing there was, what seemed to me, an elderly gentleman, in a brown dustcoat and wearing an armband with three stripes and a crown. A moment of panic as I realised what he was! I thought, "God Almighty, a flight-sergeant!" I managed to stammer an answer, "Sorry, flight-sergeant, just looking. I didn't realise they were still flying". With a hint of a smile he said, "Did you think the RAF was all flying blow-lamps. Off with you, you're keeping my lads from working with your daft questions. This lady flies but not without our help".

I left hastily, but feeling pleased. I had my first encounter with a flight-sergeant, two ranks above a corporal, and still had a head on my shoulders. Even though it was my first real day in RAF uniform I was well aware of the reputation that went with that rank. From what I had read, had seen in films and had been told, all feared the wrath of the 'Chiefies', even junior commissioned officers.

I returned to the group and Cpl Brady looked at me with narrowed eyes! He was not pleased, and said "You getting me into trouble with the chiefie", and realizing his slip of the tongue he added, "That's flight-sergeant to you, lad". He then said to me, "Interested in aeroplanes? That's handy seeing you've joined the Royal Air Force". Then, looking towards the Mosquito he said, wistfully, "Yes, that one is special. Never got the chance to fly in those".

During our break a four-engine aircraft landed and taxied close by. A first I though it was a Lancaster but realised it was the much more modern Shackelton. It must have been Shackelton engines that I heard that morning?

After the NAAFI break, our very first, we stacked our mugs to one side again and then back to the drill. A repeat of all we had done in earlier period but with Cpl Brady being much sharper in urging us to a higher standard. There was a final halt, we retrieved our mugs and headed back to the billet.

There was a definite improvement in the marching on that way back over what it had been only that few hours ago. Also we were now in three ranks instead of the two rank crocodile we had been ambling about in up to now. When we came back onto the main road of the station Cpl Brady called on Andy to take over and he went his own way. But not before he called after us, "And wash those mugs CLEAN before you go for tea. SCOUR them".

As we proceeded along the road a very smart looking uniformed gentleman hove in sight, walking along the footpath towards us. He had a peaked cap and a large silver-topped cane tucked under his arm. Even though it was a very warm evening he was wearing brown leather gloves? "Officer", I thought, expecting Andy to call "Eyes right". That didn't come? All I heard was Andy mutter, "Oh shit! The SWO!" SWO? I thought, "Oh yes, Station Warrant Officer, Warrant Officer, <u>don't</u> salute".

But I soon learn that there was good reason for Andy's alarm. As Cpl Brady had informed us on our very first meeting, on the station the SWO is God!

As we drew closer to this gentleman he stopped in his tracks, glowered towards Andy and bellowed, "WHERES YOUR CORPORAL?" "Called to SHQ, sir", Andy replied. How did Andy know that? Cpl Brady never mentioned it all afternoon? But it must have been the right answer as the SWO seemed satisfied and said nothing further.

We arrived back at the hut early and a while left before teatime. We sprawled of our beds, or 'pits', as we had quickly learned to call them. My feet were talking! The new boots had chaffed ankles and toes. Nor was I the only one suffering. 'Effing feet' or 'effing boots' were phrases used by many, up and down the bed-spaces. Whinging from the foot-sore over, discussion turned to other events of the day, in particular the foot drill. We were quiet proud of ourselves, believing we had reached a fair standard. But Andy pricked our bubble by remarking that we had a long way to go. The exercise we had gone through was just to make us less of a shambles as we moved about the station. He said, "Just wait till you start your proper 'square bashing' and do it with rifles".

A couple of comics grabbed brooms and started marching up and down the room, brooms on shoulders, to get a feel for it. In the middle of this, Cpl Brady came into the room. We all sprang to attention and stood by our beds. He looked at the two martinets' with the brooms, grinned, and said, "I'm glad you like rifle drill, you'll get sick of that very soon now, that I can guarantee."

Then he addressed us all, saying, "Listen up. You're off to really join the RAF tomorrow evening, off for Cardington." He told us we could relax for the rest of the day but get a good night's sleep as we had a lot of travelling to do in the next twenty-four hours.

Relax we did… getting our boots off as quickly as possible and off to baths and showers to ease aching feet. Then a little 'pit-bashing' then tea, followed by more 'pit-bashing' and we were refreshed for the evening. A few of us went to the cinema to see *The Halls of Montezuma*. Stirring stuff, or so it seemed then. Taking the advice of Cpl Brady all were in bed and settled before 'lights out' that evening.

~ Chapter V ~

The next morning, right on the dot of oh-eight-hundred, Cpl Brady appeared. He had good news – We would receive an advance of pay – Cheers! And bad news – We would be inspected by the SWO – Moans! Even in our very short couple of days of Service life we had learned that to have the attention of the SWO was not good news.

Cpl Brady briefed us on the rest of the days programme, "As I said you're going to RAF Cardington this evening. There you will complete induction and full scale kitting. Transport from the guardroom at seventeen-thirty to catch the Larne to Stranraer ferry. This morning, thorough clean of hut, its surrounds and the ablutions then return bedding. After lunch, SHQ, inspection by the SWO, then clearance, pack kit then early tea at sixteen-thirty, and make that a double quick scoff".

After this briefing we gave the hut it's thorough clean. 'Surrounds' was my 'room job', which involved picking up every scrap of paper and rubbish. Not a difficult job seeing it was just a few days after the Queen's visit. All I found was a few cigarette ends, and metal foil from packets, so a very easy job really, seeing there were two of us involved!

Getting the hut floor back up to the standard that would satisfy Cpl. Brady was another matter. Our boots had done damage to the gleaming state it had been when we had arrived on the first day. We all took turns at the polishing and by lunchtime we had grudging approval from Cpl Brady. I was sure it was better than we had found it but Cpl Brady did not seem to agree.

After lunch we went to SHQ for 'clearing' and inspection by the SWO. He turned out to be not nearly as fearsome as we had expected. It appeared that it was his responsibility to ensure we were fit to leave the station. He seemed unhappy with our ill-fitting uniforms, exclaiming, "J___* is there any of you normal" But we passed and it was, as the tailor had said, being left for Cardington to sort things out.

'Clearing' was just a matter of picking up temporary identification forms. We were told that our allocated Service Number was on our temporary ID form but to commit that number to memory. I learned it and never have forgotten it. We also received subsistence allowance for our journey, and joyfully received, the advance of pay! We had not, as yet, served a full week but we were given our first weeks pay, all two pounds seven shillings and sixpence (£2.33½p), if memory serves me right? We received our pay from an officer and it was our first occasion to salute! The salutes enthusiastically and gratefully given to our financial benefactor.

The subsistence allowance was about seven shillings (35p). As this was a full day's allowance we could expect a long journey ahead of us. At this stage I had just a vague idea of the whereabouts of RAF Cardington? I knew it was somewhere in the south of England and indeed a long way from RAF Aldergrove.

We then handed in our bedding and our friend Jimmy decided to be his awkward best. He closely examined every item returned, wrinkling his nose, inferring a bad smell. He accused one of our groups of cutting a piece off a blanket? Cpl Brady intervened by saying to Jimmy, "Don't be a berk, and they haven't learned that trick yet. And get a move on, we've a ferry to catch".

The 'trick' he was referring to, I later learned, was the cutting of pieces off the ends of blankets to make footpads. Movement around the hut was on these footpads in order to keep the floor in a high shine and reduce the need to polish and 'bumper'. The store staff had good reason to be suspicious of returned bedding.

Once back in the hut we packed our kit, now mostly our civilian clothes, into the kitbags. Cpl Brady suggested that we write our names somewhere on the bags and remarked that they would be properly 'stencilled' at Cardington. We would be travelling in uniform and remain in uniform for several months ahead.

When we finished packing Cpl Brady insisted on a final 'bumper' of the billet floor, to erase the fresh boot marks. We then stacked our kitbags at one end of the room and off to early tea.

As we left the dining hall we given brown paper bags containing two thick sandwiches, an apple and orange. With the lunchpack and having also receiver subsistence allowance I thought the Service was being, indeed, generous!

With tea behind us we just had enough time to collect our kit and march the couple of hundred yards to the guardroom and our transport to the ferry. Andy was put in charge and he had our travel documents. We said our goodbyes to Cpl Brady. He wished us well and we moved off. We were not long aboard the ferry before it got under way. I was leaving Ireland for the first time and to a future I had imagined but wondered what would be the reality. •

~ Chapter VI ~

It was a fine evening for our short voyage so most of us spent the time out on deck. There was an RAF sergeant also taking the air and struck up conversation with some of us. We were a bit cowed by his rank but he was a very friendly individual and put us at our ease. He knew we were recruits and gave us some very sound advice about how to face the few hard months of basic and trade training ahead of us. He said that some of us may find the basic training very hard but it was only for six weeks. We were not to think that all of our service would be like that, the real RAF we would find to be quiet different.

We were soon docking at Stranrare. We had been briefed to form up and wait in the Passenger Hall when we disembarked. A corporal met us and Andy handed him our travel papers. We were soon on a train and on our way. I noticed that the compartments had small printed window stickers, stating, 'Reserved, Armed Forces'.

It was a very long overnight journey with many stops, not all at stations, and passing through many towns and stations, the names I don't recall. The stops at stations we did have were very welcome breaks, to stretch legs and more importantly, get a vital cup of tea. Few got off at these stops but many young men both in uniform and civilian dress got on. It appeared that we were on a southbound troop-train and picking up more recruits and Servicemen along the way. At one main station, a stop near midnight, we had a longer stop and had mugs filled from tea trolleys run by the WVS (Woman's Voluntary Service) I had raided my lunch-pack several stops earlier but managed to get a chocolate bar and some biscuits from the same trolley.

We passed the journey in a variety of ways but most compartments seemed to have card games going. Even our corporal escort was engaged in a game. But no cash in view! We had been warned, strictly no gambling! There were also a few chess games on the go, being played on small travel sets.

I, like many, passed the time by reading. But I soon finished a magazine I had bought, a 'Blighty'. In those days it was a generally popular magazine devoted to cartoons, jokes, humorous articles and short stories. Some of the quiet risqué for that time and also had the obligatory 'pin-ups'. But still could be read without embarrassment in the company of the padre. It was some years later that it was renamed and became just another, top shelf in news agents, 'girlie' mag. Once read I passed my copy on to eager hands and continued with a book I had with me.

Interested in radio engineering, I had a copy of 'Foundations of Wireless' by A M Scroggie. It was a standard textbook of the time. Dry stuff and needed a fair degree of concentration to read. Good on a long journey like this as it induced sleep. But I did not sleep much as I was too interested in the passing scenes beyond the window even though I could not see much in the dark. As daylight came I saw, in quiet few fields by the side of the track, what appeared to be clusters of small ponds? I realised these were water-filled bomb craters, still there in 1953!

As we passed through towns I saw many ruined industrial sites that was obvious bomb damage. These industrial towns could also be identified by the grime on the buildings and haze of smoke hanging over them. Fumes entering the compartment as we passed through such areas signalled the nature of those heavy industries.

As I recall, it was the longest single rail journey I have ever taken. That night we travelled through a large part of Scotland and most of England! We were on that train for just over fourteen hours.

When we arrived at our final station it was full daylight again, mid morning, in fact. There seemed to be several hundred arriving for Cardington. Our corporal separated us out and formed us up outside the station. We were easily distinguished from the rest of the other arrivals; we seemed to be the only ones in uniform. Shortly, a convoy of covered trucks arrived and we were on our way again on the last stage of our journey

~ Chips for Breakfast ~

We soon arrived at, and swept through the gates of RAF Cardington. We pulled up and disembarked outside a row of huts. Black painted wooden ones exactly the same as at Aldergrove. A corporal directed us into one of the huts. It was as bare and bleak as our Aldergrove billet. But a surprise, a luxury item! On a small shelf halfway down the room, a radio! We chose bed-spaces, in the same order as Aldergrove, same people in same positions.

When we had sorted ourselves out the corporal who now appeared to be in charge of us, called for our attention and informed us of the following. For the time we were at Cardington we would be known as the 'Irish Flight' and being 'Regulars' we were to use only the 'Regular' facilities on the station. He also informed us with the very welcome news that a late breakfast had been laid on. And further good news was that having travelled overnight this day was to be a rest day. We were now to attend breakfast and then to collect our bedding. We were to be ready for inspection for oh-eight-thirty the next morning and would then receive further instructions.

We found the 'Regulars' dining hall and a small queue, it being late breakfast. The food looked not nearly as appetising as Aldergrove. I had the scrambled egg. It was lumpy, full of water, and had a bland chalky taste. The bacon was oozing white sludge and had all the flavour steamed out of it. Maybe I was tired and my taste buds below par. This stuff was, perhaps, cooked earlier this morning and now past its best. I noticed that most of our plates went to the plate-wash still with plenty on them. Perhaps we were all tired or was I being too optimistic about the food.

Soon after we returned from breakfast and airman appeared, an SAC (Senior Aircraftsman). He was visibly startled when we all sprang to attention and stood up by our beds. Recovering from his surprise he asked us to follow him to collect our bedding. The bedding store was only a few huts away and we were soon back and beds made up.

Although the beds looked inviting, properly made up now with clean sheets and pillowcase, none us seemed tired enough to want to get into them. Most of us went for a wash and shave, showers or baths. We had been fully dressed for over twenty-four hours now so a bath or shower was very welcome. After which we all just sat around and talked and generally relaxed.

Someone turned on the radio and tuned to some popular music of the day. Most of us lay on our beds. I soon dozed off. I was awakened, sometime later, by someone rattling irons on a mug and loudly proclaiming it to be lunchtime. But I was still ballasted by the late breakfast so I, and quiet a few others decided to give lunch a miss. Towards tea time we stirred ourselves, had a wash and freshen up and did partake of that meal. I was now hungry enough to be indifferent to its quality, but as I can recall, that meal was not at all bad.

Now evening, discussion turned to how to spent the time. Most of us opted to find the NAAFI. Others, undecided, lay on their beds listening to the radio. As we of the NAAFI bound party were about to leave a corporal we had not seen before came into the room.

We all leaped to our feet and stood to attention by our beds. Like the SAC of earlier, the corporal looked every bit as startled but got over his surprise and asked, "Who are you lot". When we chorused, "The Irish Flight" his expression changed to horror! He made straight for the radio, switched it off, unplugged it and left the room with the radio without a further word. We never saw that corporal, or the radio, for the rest of our stay at Cardington? Nor did we learn what might have inspired such a reaction? Deprived of radio as entertainment a few more joined our group in the quest for the NAAFI.

The NAAFI buildings were the other side of some open ground opposite our hut. Crossing this open ground we saw it was equipped as an assault course. We tried a few of the obstacles on our way but the need for refreshment called.

A sign above the door of the NAAFI building indicated that it was the 'NAAFI Club, Regular Airmen' For some reason the 'powers' had decided that new entrant 'regulars' and 'national service' should be kept apart. The reason was never explained. We were also segregated by title. The 'regulars' were referred to as

Regular Service Airmen, or Volunteers, and 'national service' as NSAs (National Service Airmen).

In the NAAFI we had tea or soft drinks and then decided to watch TV. Here on mainland UK the reception was good. A clear and steady picture on a large screen projection set. The picture was black and white picture and just a single channel, the BBC.

We watched TV for a couple of hours. I cannot remember what the programmes were about but it must have been interesting to keep us watching. But then it was a great novelty for we bogtrotters, having seen TV for the very first time, only days before.

After the TV viewing session we had supper in NAAFI. Fish and chips with orange juice!? Although all of us were old enough to have alcohol none of us did. However, as I have already mentioned, most seemed to smoke. The atmosphere in the TV room and here in the canteen was thick with smoke as it was at Aldergrove.

We returned to the hut before 10 pm (Sorry, twenty-two-hundred-hours) and were well settled down by 'lights out' at twenty-three hundred hours. No chitchat and banter after lights-out that particular evening, but a sudden silence and soon all asleep.

Next morning I slept through to reveille, awakened by the tannoy. The ablutions were very busy when I got there and had to wait my turn for a washbasin. While waiting I found it strange to hear all the different accents. Every region of the British Isles seemed to be represented in that morning gathering. Mostly cheerful voices but also a few gloomy faces. Many, it seemed, were National Service, starting two years of a life not of their choosing.

After breakfast, happily, of a better standard than the day before, we cleaned and tidied the room the best we could with the only cleaning equipment available. That comprised of two well-used and partially bald brooms.

The corporal, who had dealt with us on our arrival the previous day, appeared just after oh-eight-thirty. He did a cursory inspection and seemed satisfied in spite of the standard being far below that at Aldergrove. He informed us that we would now to go 'Stores' to receive the remainder or our kit. We were instructed to take our 'civvies' and kit bags with us. We formed up outside the hut and marched off.

The Station Clothing Stores here at Cardington was massive. The counter seemed to go on forever and there were acres of shelves and racking behind them and an army of staff dealing with issues. It was here that we received the balance, and bulk, of our kit. Issue was speedy and efficient and without the grudging and drama we had experienced at Aldergrove. Here at Cardington it was a very professional supply system, run by staff used to issuing thousands of items each day.

The issues included webbing and 'accoutrements'. Belt, cross-straps, large pack, small pack, ammunition pouches, water bottle and bayonet frog. All this in strong blue-grey canvas with brass buckles, hooks and tabs. Standard army infantry issue, in fact, except for the colour. It had changed very little in design since WWI.

Also issued was a 'groundsheet' in green rubberised material. This was a multipurpose item designed and intended as a rain cape but it could serve also as a lean-to bivouac and, of course, a groundsheet. I had one of these at home. War surplus, sold as and used as a cycle cape.

Later, and more than once, I was to hear of another purpose for the groundsheet. It was issued to airmen to prevent members of WRAF from getting rheumatism? I was also to hear, in barrack room banter, the WRAF, or some members in particular, unkindly referred to as 'groundsheets'!

We were issued with the rest of our uniform and other kit items such as mess tins, boot, shoe and clothes brushes and button-stick. Also one handy little item, the subject of many poor jokes, a 'housewife', pronounced 'hussuff'. This was a sewing kit comprising a little linen pouch containing needles, thread, spare uniform buttons and darning wool. It seems that we were required to keep uniform in good repair by self-help. That item and the brushes, I still have. The brushes have served me well and later my family. Still in use and showing little sign of wear after the best part of fifty years.

We were taken in hand by a posse of tailors, who measured and chalked our ill-fitting No. 2 Blues. We then changed into the very creased No.1 blues (Number One Home Dress) just issued and the measuring and chalking process was repeated. The tailor who measured me up smiled and shook his head when he saw the amount that my 'blues' would have to be taken up in the waist. He remarked, "They should put you on double rations, I could run up another (uniform) with what I will take up in this".

The greatcoat proved less of problem as I got one that was a close fit when worn over No. 1 blue! After fitting we wrote our Service numbers and names on the labels in the uniform items. We then changed into our now very creased 'civvies' and handed over our uniforms for alteration.

We then took the rest of our kit to what appeared to be a workshop. There, all items were stencilled or stamped with our Service numbers. Then it was back to the hut, with full kitbags and festooned webbing. The kitbag now stencilled with our number and name in two-inch high black characters

Back in our bed-spaces we examined our new acquisitions and surveyed the webbing with some bewilderment? It was just a tangle or straps and buckles. But with the help of Andy and our corporal we made sense of it. And learned the purpose of the assorted bits and how to link them all up to make coherent whole.

We also learned that there were rules as to what went into the 'small (side) pack' and the 'large (back) pack. We were told not to worry about the mouldy canvas and green 'brasses' as 'square bashing' would soon sort that out. We removed the worst of the mould and dust with a hard brush. Once all the parts were buckled and hooked up together it formed an integral harness and could be slipped on or off simply by hasping and unhasping the belt. We practiced webbing assembly and kit packing until teatime.

After tea we just lay on our beds, indulging in a little 'pit bashing'. Later, most of us elected to go to the station cinema. There was a massive queue when we arrived and here again it seems that privilege of rank and status prevailed. As in the dining halls, NCOs and other staff could go to the head of the queue with mere recruits the very last in the pecking order! But it was a large cinema, housed in part of a hanger sized building. The show had started by the time we got seated. I can remember that event in great detail but the title of the film and whether or not it was worth queuing for, escapes me? •

~ Chapter VII ~

Our first activity, immediately after breakfast the next morning, was an extended room cleaning session. Cleaning materials, including bumpers, had made an appearance. However, even our best efforts did not bring the floor up to the standard of our Aldergrove hut. But then, Cardington did not have the benefit of a visit from the Queen and the 'all stops out' preparation there must have been for that event. Cardington was a transit camp with hundreds passing through each week, so standards reflected this situation.

The tailors must have worked overtime and a night shift because immediately after the cleaning session we revisited the Clothing Stores to collect our altered No. 2 blues. And now they did fit! I could tuck my beret into my waistband without it vanishing it down inside my trousers!

We were told to get them pressed and to keep them smart, and clean, as we would be on 'special duties' at the weekend? 'Special duties'? It sounded mysterious. But as it turned out that weekend was to be RAF Cardington's 'Battle of Britain' Open Day, and we, still untrained recruits, were to be let loose on the public in an effort to provide some assistance?

We were also required to help with the preparations for the Open Day. When our corporal was allocating the various tasks he asked if anyone had any knowledge of aircraft? The whole room pointed at me, and two others. We three, it seemed, had been boring everyone to death, airing our knowledge of aircraft! We three were to report to the Education Section to help in setting up their displays. We wondered how this task could have any connection with aircraft?

But on reporting for duty at the Education Section we discovered that there was a connection. Many of the items being put on display were very detailed scale model aircraft, both those in current service and from World War II and earlier. Some of the models were quiet large, with cut-away sections showing the innards and workings in great detail. Fascinating to me, having only seen such detail before in books and magazines and more recently, in 'Eagle' comic. Our corporal and hut-mates may have thought that this task was a little joke on we three 'plane spotters', but we could not have been more pleased.

Our job was to unpack the models from their special fitted crates and set them up on stands. I opened one crate and was startled to see it contained a sinister looking torpedo shaped object with tail fins! It was a 250lb bomb. Just another training model with cutaway sections to show its inner workings.

Once the exhibition was completely set up the education officer inspected and pronounced it to be to his satisfaction. He thanked us for our efforts and informed us that we would be required to assist with the public on the Open Day.

In the meantime, I, and most of the Irish Flight were required to attend Trade Selection. For reasons never explained we were, once again, put through the full selection process, as we had in Belfast.

On completing the aptitude tests I was informed that all RAF trades were open to me but again the technical trades required enlistment for a minimum of ten years? To my dismay I was told that Motorboat Crew was now a closed trade! I would have to make another choice if I wished to serve only for five years. But there was not much to choose from? I was faced with the same limited choice as I had been given at Belfast, which now excluded Motorboat Crew. I could clearly see that to enter a trade that I really wanted my only option was to enlist for ten years.

I made that decision and was given a fresh application form to complete and enter my new trade choices. I was given a short while to think it over and was supplied with a pile of literature on all the various RAF trades. My first choice was again was my original first choice, Wireless Operator. My second choice was Wireless Mechanic. As a third choice, and on a whim, I entered Radar Operator. That particular trade had not been mentioned before and seemed interesting, even from the sparse information I had now been given.

The completed form was taken away and I was asked to wait to be interviewed concerning my new trade choices. The waiting area was an anti-room, sparsely furnished but with the walls practically covered in posters and pictures of the many and varied RAF trades and activities. Again, as in the literature, lots of smiling faces in sunny places. Very sunny places in many instances, seeing that those depicted were in tropical dress. But smiles were in short supply among those waiting to be interviewed. It was like a dentists waiting room with a dozen or more sitting in nervous silence. I was in a mild shock, having now committed myself to ten years of service!

My thoughts were interrupted when I thought I heard my name called? The call was repeated, but louder, "AC O'REILLY!" I then realised it was me being called for but it was the first time I had been addressed by the rank of AC (Aircraftsman). So far I had been addressed as 'Recruit' or just 'lad'.

The call had come from one of offices off the waiting area. The slightly ajar door had a sign showing the occupant's rank as sergeant but I cannot recall the name. I went in and there, indeed, behind a desk was a sergeant who looked and sounded very like the jovial character of the Belfast office. He smiled as I entered and said, "Sit down, sit down" gesturing towards the vacant chair in front of his desk. I sat down. He studied a form on his desk and muttered, "Good, good, uh-hu, uh-hu", in an approving manner. I gathered that he must have been studying my newly completed form.

He then raised his head, looked at me, and said, "I see you are planning to make the Royal Air Force your career". Exactly the same words I had heard at Belfast but now that I was going for a ten-year stretch I suppose it would be a career. I answered, "Yes, I am signing on for ten years to get a good trade". He responded, "A yes, a very good trade, Radar Operator". "Radar Operator!" was my surprised thought? I pointed out that Radar Operator was my third choice but he quickly came back with, "Ah yes, your third choice, but your best choice, a wise choice".

He then went on to explain that 'Radar Operator' was a relatively new trade, which was being expanded, so the opportunity for promotion was very good. He stated, "Very short of NCOs in that trade. The way things are you could be a corporal in less that two years and a sergeant in, maybe, three years. Great range of postings too, lots overseas"

He went on, pointing to his rank chevrons on one sleeve, "Just think, in as short a time as three years you could have these up, and be on nearly seven quid (£7) a week". I was impressed, and now convinced that that although Radar Operator had been my third choice, and a whim, it probably had been my best choice!

I returned to the hut with mixed feelings. On one hand I was happy with my new trade and hopeful for my future in the RAF, but also very aware that I had signed away ten years of my life. I would have to inform my parents of the change in circumstances. No longer would it be a short term of service to 'make a man of me' and learn a trade. Their fledgling had now, without doubt, 'flown the coop'.

The next day was taken up with the final preparations for the Open Day. We were to be in 'No. 2 blues for the event and were duly inspected to make sure we were up to standard to appear before the public. We passed muster but with constructive criticism and suggested improvements. We also had a final brief on our duties in the education section and had to mug up on information relating the exhibits. The latter should enable us to give some kind of intelligent answer to possible questions by visitors. Four of us had been allocated to this duty. Two would do a morning session and two the afternoon. That arrangement allowed us time to see the rest of the Open Day show. I was detailed for the morning stint.

I reported for my first RAF working duty at oh-eight-thirty on the Open Day morning in a well-pressed 'blue' and polished cap badge. There were several of us reporting and we were inspected by a sergeant. He seemed satisfied with our turnout, but had this to say to us, "I know you are recruits, but try not to sound too stupid if you are asked any questions you can't answer. Don't waffle. Come to me or the flight-lieutenant, if you get stuck".

There was no great rush of visitors to our contribution. The more interesting exhibits and demonstrations were taking place in and around the two huge hangers that are a feature of RAF Cardington. We did have a steady trickle or visitors but not many questions were put to us. Most of the visitors we did have seemed to know a lot more than we did. Most of the school age children seemed to have an impressive knowledge of aircraft.

Many of the adult visitors seemed to have served through the war and had first hand knowledge of many of the older aircraft on display. One gentleman did query me thus, "What can you tell me of this one, son?" He enquired, nodding towards one of the World War II model aircraft. "That's a 'Wimpey', sir", I answered, airing my knowledge by using the more common name for the Wellington bomber. I carried on further with the basic technical details that I knew of this aircraft. He nodded, smiled, then prodded a gun turret on the model with his finger and said, "Spent many frozen hours it that thing, then we went down and in the bag for three years. Be glad that's all well in the past before you joined". He then moved on. But I understood from his remarks that he had been an air-gunner, and had been shot down and spent three years as a POW. I would genuinely have liked to hear his full story.

I have since met many who served during the war but found very few who saw real combat willing to talk of their experience. Even when pressed they will only impart snippets. You have to know them well and to get nearly the full story. Such has been my experience. Then there are those, well known, who made a career out of their war experience. But I am grateful for their books and stories and don't doubt the great contribution they have made to recorded history. By writing this I suppose have I joined that 'band wagon' but I very much doubt what I have written will ever be sought out by students of history.

My stint as guide and oracle on matters aeronautical ended at lunchtime. The sergeant thanked us, saying we had done well considering we had not yet completed basic training. As a reward we were given a 'bonus, an Evening Pass! It would allow us off the station until twentythree-fiftynine hours (one minute to midnight).

But that freedom was subject to my No. 1 'blue' and greatcoat passing inspection. We had only received them back from the tailors the pervious afternoon, very creased and still with the remnants of the chalk marks, and the buttons green with corrosion!

I had a very quick lunch and then back to the hut to make a start on getting my kit in a fit state to allow me past the Guardroom. But I did not want to miss the Open Day show so hoped to complete my uniform 'bulling up' later.

On leaving the hut I made straight for the hanger where most of interesting features of the Open Day were being put on. Most of what was on display and featured was concerned with parachute training. That was a major function of Cardington in those days. The school used one hanger and it was rumoured that the second hanger still housed the wreck of the ill-fated airship, R101.

Visitors could try out many of the parachute training apparatus. One I had to try was jumping from a thirty-foot tower. In a parachute harness attached to a braked line, of course, to control the rate of decent. Nevertheless, the drop was at a realistic rate and a hair-raising experience. I was happy to have tried it just once. However, there was seemed to be reluctance for members of the public to have a go. The sergeant supervising this feature hijacked me and had me make repeated jumps to encourage others? After I had made several jumps and had not broken legs or neck, thankfully a queue did form. I then made my escape, feeling light headed and convinced I was now several inches shorter.

Another feature in the hanger was a balloon ride for the kiddies. A barrage balloon had a large basket slung beneath it. The kiddies could board the basket and ascend to the hanger roof. Ascent and decent was controlled by attached lines. To make the ride more interesting the operators swayed the basket by swinging on the lines. I noticed that one of our Irish Flight lads was operating a line.

As I was watching these capers the public address announced that a parachute display as about to begin so I decided to go and watch the professionals make a jump. The display was being performed by trainee paratroops, jumping from the captive balloon used in normal training. The gondola carried about six including an RAF instructor.

The gondola was loaded up amid great barking of orders from the Parachute Regiment sergeant in charge of the trainees. The balloon ascended, stopped at height of several hundred feet and hovered there. I thought that they were surely not going to jump from that low? But the balloon was winched down unloaded and the winch truck moved to a new position. We were informed that the wind had veered and the repositioning was to avoid the parachutists landing among the spectators.

The parachutes in use were World War II military style, without the glide control and steering of modern chutes. Once the jump was made, it was straight down and at the mercy of the wind with the very minimum of directional control.

With the winch truck repositioned the balloon again ascended and the jump took place, all exiting the gondola in very quick succession. The sergeant was first out, identified by his shouting. He barked at the rest of the 'stick' all the way down. He, of course, made a perfect landing and continued bawling at the trainees without, it seemed, a pause for breath.

One of the trainees made a bad landing and was dragged along the ground, his canopy remaining filled by the wind. Straight towards where I was standing and I was soon enveloped in parachute. I, and other spectators grabbed the canopy to collapse it but the sergeant yelled, "Don't help him, he's got to learn. Stand back". We stood back and the hapless trainee was dragged off the grassed field and yards across the tarmac road edging the field. The sergeant snapping at his heels all the way.

As it transpired, the trainee had been hurt on landing and could not stand up to collapse and release his parachute. He was taken away by ambulance to applause from the crowd.

At the end of the parachute display the rest of the small troop took a bow, also to loud applause. When the sergeant came to take his separate bow there was an outbreak of booing and hissing from the crowd. But that was all in good humour and quickly turned to laughter and cheering.

After the parachute display I visited an exhibit that was a 'must' for me. That was a mobile radar system. The Decca Company was showing this new equipment. I joined the queue and was soon being shown the displays and having the details explained. I had only ever seen photographs and film of radar before and was impressed by this equipment even though it was short range, designed for airfield use.

The Decca representative explained everything in great detail. He related the green smudges on displays, traced by the radar, to actual features and landmarks in the surrounding landscape. There was a completely blank sector for nearly a quarter of the display. This was explained as a 'cone of silence' produced by a 'radar shadow, cast by the large hangers so close by. However, the responses we could see were just confused smudges to me, making me apprehensive about becoming a radar operator? But that was still in the future and just surviving 'square-bashing' was the uppermost thought in my mind.

After I had seen all I had time to see, I rushed back to the hut to continue my uniform 'bull' session. It would take some time and effort to get my No. 1 blue and greatcoat into a state that would get me past the guardroom. The tailors had did their job in getting them to an acceptable fit but it would need a lot of pressing to pass muster.

The brass buttons were crusted in verdigris and getting them to an acceptable standard would not be easy. On route to the hut I met up with other members of the Irish Flight, in equal haste. It appeared that I was not the only one given the privilege of an evening pass!

When we entered the hut some were already there and frantically beavering away, polishing and pressing. The whole Flight, it seems, had evening passes! It transpired that in view of our time in uniform, short though that was our mini square-bash at Aldergrove had persuaded the 'powers' at Cardington that we could be let loose for a evening.

There was also another reason, and possibly the real reason, for being given passes for that particular evening! It was to allow us to attend the showing of a new film in the local town of Bedford. The film was 'The Red Beret', the story of the forming of the Parachute Regiment and some of their wartime exploits. Some scenes had been shot at Cardington, making use of the parachute school facilities.

The famous Commando raid on the German radar station at Brunaval, in which the RAF had some involvement, was featured it the film. It was therefore considered to be of some 'educational and training value'. Servicemen attending the cinema in uniform would be admitted at much reduced price. We had heard that some complimentary tickets were available on the station but none of those came our way.

Not all of the Flight was enthused by the prospect an evening of freedom and a film show. It appeared that many were now broke and could not afford the few shillings the evening out would cost. The two pounds odd they had received at Aldergrove had, literally, gone up in smoke or across the NAAFI bar counter. I had a small reserve of a few shillings left so I was definitely going out.

For those of us going off station, money was not the problem, but getting our uniforms up to the standard that would allow us past the Guardroom was. So now it was matter of frantic polishing and pressing. There was a queue for the single iron and pressing our uniforms was fairly simple matter once we got hands on the iron. However, getting those green buttons to as acceptable shine took the time and effort. The verdigris did indeed prove stubborn to remove from the crowns and eagles on the buttons. However, someone had the forethought to have acquired a brass bristled suede brush. That was passed around and made short shift of the verdigris! But we still had to forgo going to tea in order get the job done.

As we were in the midst of these preparations the last few on Open Day duties entered the billet. One chap, it seemed, had a really bad day! He whipped off his beret and flung it forcibly onto his bed, exclaiming, "F___ing kids. Lukit me, lukit me blue"! We looked. His uniform jacket was streaked and spotted as if he had received the attention of a large bird. A very large bird! Someone remarked, "Seagull" To which our irate chum replied, "Seagull, shite, I've been honked on from a great height!" He had been one of the line operators on the barrage balloon kiddie ride and one of the children had shown appreciation by being airsick on top of him! •

~ Chapter VIII ~

It was a warm September evening, too warm for greatcoats, but we were required to carry them! And to carry them in the prescribed manned, neatly folded, buttons fastened and outwards on display. 'The coat carried over the left arm and the arm to be kept smartly at the horizontal, at all times', so said the rules. Getting them folded properly was a feat in itself. But when finally ready we made our way, hopefully, towards the guardroom

When we arrived, there was a long and painfully slow moving queue. An RAF policeman was carrying out a minute inspection of every airman in the queue! My heart sank as I saw some being turned away. My turn came. Buttons were peered at, even having to show the ones hidden on the folds of my greatcoat. Having looked me over I was very relieved when the police corporal said, "Pass". I was about to move on but the corporal bellowed, "YOUR PASS, STUPID"! I got the messaged and proffered my Evening Pass form. He looked at it very closely as if it were a suspect banknote, then handed it back, grunted and waved me on. I got the feeling that he was disappointed that all was in order.

I then had to join another queue at the guardroom window in order to 'book out' That consisted of entering our Service details in a large ruled book, writing in the last three digits of our Service number, then our rank, name and initials, sign and record our time out as shown by the guardroom clock. Only then were we free to proceed on out through the gate.

We then joined yet another queue for the bus, at the stop near the gate. It was a long queue and I wondered if we would all get onboard the bus. As we waited, I, and others, were startled by a shout from the guardroom, "THAT MAN! YOU THERE, SMOKING, COME HERE!" The offender left the bus queue and back to the guardroom. He had not rejoined us by the time the bus came. Smoking in public, in uniform, was another 'no-no'. At least there was now one less for the bus. But two came and we all managed to pile on. It appeared that this was a special effort because of the film show.

A few had tried to push to the head of the bus queue, claiming the staff privilege, but were quickly thwarted by an older recruit, displaying medal ribbons. He bellowed at the queue-jumpers, "OY, YOU'R OFF THE STATION NOW, MATES, NO PRIVILAGES HERE"! Whether he was right, or not, they didn't argue, but meekly went to the back of the queue to a mummer of approval form all others assembled.

I enjoyed the film, even with a cowboy in the leading role! That part played by Alan Ladd, who I had previously seen only in 'Westerns'. In 'TheRed Beret' he played the part of a Canadian, so his American accent in a British war film was acceptable. I supposed that by having an American in a leading role the makers had an eye the United States, and a wider market. British made films, and there were not many then, were mostly made for home consumption.

At that time many in the American forces regarded the beret as an article of ridicule, a point brought out in the film. Yet, less than ten years later, to wear the beret in the American forces was to be among the elite. Because of my parachuting experience from that morning, I viewed the film with the swelled-headed notion that I now had some expertise in the subject?

Once out of the cinema after the show and into the cool night, the hunger pangs struck. My missing tea meal was now most definitely being missed. I, and the other few that had tagged along together, followed our noses and found a 'Chippies'. There was nearly always a fish and chip shop close to a cinema, often right next door, or so it seemed, in those days.

We each treated ourselves to a mound of chips, a large portion of crispy battered cod. Liberally salted and splashed with white vinegar, all wrapped in newspaper. We also indulged in a bottle of 'pop' each and still had change out of a two bob (10p) piece. And that included a small charge of two pence (¾p approx) for the pop bottle. Hunger thus satisfied we caught the bus back to camp.

We must have reeked from the fish and chips, judging by the looks we got from other passengers and the conductress. However, as the bus was almost totally full of RAF recruits the distinct odour from all the new uniforms more or less overwhelmed the aroma of our fish and chips.

We booked back in at the guardroom well before the one-minute to midnight deadline. As it was a Saturday night we had the privilege of 'extended lights 'so we avoided having to stumble about in the dark when we arrived back at the hut.

On the following day, Sunday, we all attended church service in the morning and the afternoon was spent in the clearing up after the Open Day.

First thing on Monday we attended a photographic session, for our proper RAF Identity Cards. The little blue card, with our photograph, service details and official stamp, so familiar to all RAF Servicemen, the Form 1250. Seldom referred to as an ID card but most always, simply called a 'twelve-fifty'.

When issued with the cards we were told to regard our 1250s as a £5 note, a fortune to us then. That, we were told, would be the cost of replacement, plus also being put on a charge, if we lost it. We were also told that now in possession of our 1250s we were fully inducted members of the Royal Air Force and could be put on a charge. We would be required to show our 1250s to anyone in authority, on demand. We received this news with both pride and apprehension.

That same afternoon the corporal in charge told us that a civilian photographer would be around to take group and individual photographs. We were to be in number one 'blue' and SD caps. No bare heads, but berets could be worn with 'number ones' on this occasion. This rule bending, I supposed, to increase sales of photographs.

The photographer duly arrived, a lady with a large camera on a tripod. Most of the Flight had photos taken, individual and in small groups. But for a few, the price of one shilling and sixpence (7.5p) for a postcard size print was still too much for some! Among those having photos takes some wore their berets, claiming that the beret looked smarter than the peaked SD (Service Dress) 'bus conductor's' hat.

When we returned to the hut after the private photo session our corporal informed us that we would be on the 'basic training draft' the day after tomorrow. The next morning we would have a full kit inspection and then pack all but for immediate needs. We would also have a 'pay parade' and that bit of news greeted whistles and cheers. Another cash injection was indeed very sorely needed by many. A lot of us had been donating our last bits of change to be shut up the whining and relieve the misery of our smoking pals.

We our kit inspection the next morning was carried out by a very young pilot-officer, accompanied by a sergeant. The main concern being that we were up to scale in kit, still had all items issued and nothing was defective. We were told that we would we travelling the next day in 'number-ones' and as it was still Summer Order Dress we were to pack away our greatcoats. Webbing was to be made up to fit properly over our No. 1 blues.

After the inspection our corporal instructed us in the art of proper packing of kitbags and webbing packs. We were shown the best way to pack in the interests of kit care, comfort and smartness. The accent was on smartness and how to achieve properly 'squared 'packs and a properly packed, cylindrical and rigid kitbag. Having it properly packed and rigid, the kitbag could be balanced and carried on top of the also rigid well 'squared' backpack.

We were also told to give our water bottles a thorough wash and fill them with fresh water in the morning.

After a period of practice packing and adjusting of webbing, we were given some instruction on how to conduct ourselves on pay parade. We had been taken through that drill at Aldergrove, but our corporal now in charge, ran through it again to make sure we had it right; Listen for name and 'last three' called - respond by calling 'last three' and 'SIR', step smarty out of line - <u>march</u> up to pay table - come to attention - salute – sign (smartly?). Collect pay - salute - about turn and <u>march</u> back to place in the Flight – step smartly back into line. All that and we had not yet had basic training! After we all did a 'dummy run' our corporal was satisfied that we had a grasp of the drill, we were marched off.

The pay parade was held in a large hall and there seemed to be hundreds in attendance! However, there were also a number of pay tables, each manned by an officer and an SNCO. I had to listen very carefully for my name being called because of all the shouting and stamping of feet echoing around the hall.

We were called in alphabetical order, so it took ages for my name to be called. If this is how pay parades were always to be conducted I was glad that my father had readopted the 'O' prefix to our name. If still named Reilly it would have taken a lot longer. I thought that if this happens every two weeks in the Service with thousands of men wasting thousands of hours to get their pay, there must be a better way.

For any who served in the RAF during the fifties and sixties will remember; it was over twenty years later before all ranks had bank accounts. But it also took that time for all ranks to gain a pay rate worth banking. Before that it was often the case of pay on Friday, broke by Monday!

But we of the 'Irish Flight' were in for a shock! Having been paid in advance at Aldergrove we just received a small amount of subsistence allowance for our impending journey. Our next full payment would not be until a week later at RAF Bridgenorth.

The pay parade took nearly two hours and then we returned to the hut to finish our packing. All the smokers, most on the Flight, were in a state of shock. We had to listen to at least half an hour of expletives and moans of despair as the addicted vented their disappointment.

Then to add insult to injury our corporal suggested that we should invest in 'D rings' to secure our kitbags. 'D rings' were hinged curved metal rings that threaded through the eyelets of the kitbag and is secured with a padlock. It was no surprise to learn that the NAAFI stocked these items. But as soon as the corporal had left the room it became clear as to what he should do with the suggestion.

A few of us already had these items as they were in common use to secure cycles. However, in spite of the universally declared poverty, others did acquire 'D' rings.

The hut that evening sounded as if we had an infestation of crickets such was the clicking and clattering of the metal 'D rings'. They proved, in fact, to be a handy device as they effectively closed and secured the kitbag, and also provided a convenient rigid handle.

That last evening, before departing Cardington, a few of us decided to satisfy our curiosity about the NSA NAAFI Club. Was it in anyway different from that of the 'Regulars'? We went in and found that there was no immediately apparent difference? It looked exactly the same even down to the pattern of the wallpaper. We decided to try the TV room. There were two airmen standing by the door.

As we tried to enter one of the airmen said, "Ninepence lads, admission"! This was different; TV was free in the 'Regulars' NAAFI! We elected not to part with our cash and go for the cheaper option of a cup of tea. As we were being served we were discussing the matter of having to pay to watch TV. The NAAFI lady serving us must have overheard, and called out, "Miss Thompson, those 'wide boys' are at it again"! We gathered from this that the TV admission charge was a scam, but by the time 'Miss Thompson' (NAAFI Manageress, I supposed) appeared, the 'wide boys' had vanished! It appeared to be a common scam and perpetrators could quickly collect enough for a few beers from gullible recruits.

After breakfast the next morning we returned our bedding and that followed by a final hut cleaning and inspection. Andy was not joining us but going his separate way. He was going direct to 'refresher' training.

Although it had been really only days ago since we all met up we felt we were parting from an old friend. We said out farewells and thanked him for his help. The culture shock of our first couple of weeks in the Service I am sure had been made much easier by having had Andy in our midst.

We then formed up outside in full kit we were given a final inspected. Close attention being to proper adjustment of webbing.

Water bottles were scrutinised to ensure we had cleaned and filled them as instructed. We were then marched off through the camp and into open fields.

At the near end of the field there were several lines of trestle tables piled high with brown paper wrapped packages. These were pack-lunches, our rations for the trip. They were the same style and uniform RAF lunch-packs as we had received at Aldergrove. Others ahead of me, having received their rations, were crossing the field in an extended line and making towards a waiting train. RAF Cardington had it's own railway station, albeit just an open platform, since its heyday as a major airship station.

Having received my lunch-pack and in my hurry to catch up, I passed between two corporals. They were standing close to together with their backs to me. There should have been enough room but I had forgotten about the kitbag astride my backpack. The corporal on my left received the end of the kitbag on the back of his neck. He was not pleased, and said so, in the best NCO fashion! My mental and physical ability, and parentage, all called into question. I was glad at that I was leaving and not arriving.

I boarded the train, a special troop train. There must have been at least two hundred of us in the in the draft, all those from the pay parade the previous day, now all heading for RAF Bridgnorth. It was a corridor train, eight to a compartment and seats for all, but with all our webbing and packs not a lot of spare space. Fortunately, our kitbags had been put in the guards van. We divested of our webbing and managed to, more or less, stow it all in the overhead luggage racks.

Two other members of the Irish Flight were among those in my compartment. We were soon all talking and speculating on the whereabouts of Bridgnorth and how long it might take us to get there. I hadn't a clue as to where it might be. My knowledge of the geography of England at that time was limited to the location of major towns and cities, but of smaller locations I had no idea. One of our travelling companions said that Bridgnorth was near Wolverhampton. Which was not a lot of help. We knew of its famous football team but had only a vague idea of the location of the town itself.

As to arrival time we had no idea. The train got under way as just after 10am and as we had been given rations we assumed that the journey would be at least a few hours. But some hours later and time to dig into the lunch-packs we were still meandering through the countryside. A mug of tea would have gone down well with the sandwiches but all we had to drink was the now tepid water in our bottles. We passed through many stations, names meaningless and not remembered.

Eventually we stopped at a main station. We spotted tea trolleys on the platform and there was a general scramble to get to the very much desired, and needed, refreshment. But hardly had our fastest set a boot on the platform when NCOs and RAF police appeared in droves, yelling in hoarse chorus, "GET BACK ON THE TRAIN". Having corralled us again they had their mugs filled, and re-boarded the train. We had stopped just long enough to see to the comforts of the shepherds, but not the sheep.

It was a warm day and the compartment stuffy, which brought on thirst. The remaining contents of my water bottle did nothing for this thirst. The water was by this time, warm and laden with breadcrumbs, the residue from my lunch. I had several leg stretches by walking the corridor. There were card games in full swing in nearly every other compartment and singing in some. Someone was playing a harmonica.

The songs were mostly old ones, including 'Lillie Marlene' and 'Tipperary'. Here was another generation, now in uniform, singing the songs of their fathers and grandfathers. I imagined for a moment, how it might have been for my grandfather, setting off for France in 1914, in hope and innocence? But I was merely on my way to basis training and I should survive that. He was killed in October 1914, at Givenchy, a small battle that gets little mention in the history of WWI.

Back in the present, here on the train, the singing had changed to Rugby songs, A raucous voice started singing 'The Virgin

Sturgeon' and this was taken up and sung by most in the carriage, if not the whole train.

We trundled on for hours making frequent stops in the middle of nowhere. It seems that troop trains have a very low traffic priority, so our journey was slow. But eventually the train pulled into a station and cheering broke out. That started at the front and progressed down the length of the train in a vocal 'Mexican wave'. I looked out to see the station sign. It read 'Bridgnorth'. We had, at last, arrived. It was late afternoon, insofar as I can remember. •

~ Chapter IX ~

All the merriment came to a sudden end as the train came to a halt. No sooner had it stopped than the bellowing and barking started. Corporals everywhere, yelling, "OFF THE TRAIN' LINE UP IN TWOS"! We scrabbled around for our kit, got harnessed back into webbing and scrambled off the train.

Line up in twos? They were expecting a lot from untrained rabble! However, after much milling about and almost hysterical yelling from the corporals we formed up in fairly orderly lines along the length of the platform. We then collected our kitbags from the tangled heap where they had been unceremoniously dumped on the platform. When we had formed up again a sergeant worked down the line, counting off groups. A corporal then shepherded off each group, continuously yapping at heels, to waiting trucks.

It was like a chaotic sheep-dog trial with we blue clad and webbing festooned beings playing the sheep. But I could see now that it was the sergeants that were the shepherds and the corporals the sheep dogs. But when you are a sheep the dog is master. These particular NCOs, like the RAF police, were another special breed. We had been delivered into the clutches of a species known as Drill Instructors (DIs).

My group clambered onto our assigned truck, filling the bench seats down each side and some standing. I had a seat but it was probably more comfortable if standing as hunched forward because of our backpacks we all looked decidedly constipated. A corporal had boarded the truck, our escort, commandeering a seat by the tailboard and we moved off in convoy.

With the stern faced corporal, looking every inch a guard, for the second time in two weeks I felt more like a POW than a 'volunteer in Her Majesty's service'. With all the hustle, shouting and shepherding on and off trains, I had a darker thought. I was reminded a little of the terrible images of the poor 'Holocaust' victims that I had seen in cinema newsreels in the late 1940s. All that was missing were the dogs but the DIs barked just as loudly and seemed every bit as vicious.

But that was just a fleeting thought, as I knew that to move masses of men there was little room for individual treatment or polite requests. I had to accept that I was no longer an individual, but a very small cog in a very large machine. AC2 stood for Aircraftsman Second Class, so for time being, I was going to have to accept being regarded as a lower life form.

Our kitbags came in handy on this journey. Jammed between our knees they prevented us from falling forward on our faces as the truck took some sharp curves.

It was a short journey from the railway station and we were very soon though the main gates of RAF Bridgnorth.

It seemed a very smart and imposing gateway with two very smart looking sentries on duty. They seemed so smart and military-like that it did not occur to me that they too were trainees.

Our truck pulled up outside a group of huts and after another short session of bellowing and organised bedlam I found myself in possession of a bed-space, with bed and mattress, pillows two, small locker, large locker (wardrobe) and was standing by the bed.

Each mattress and pillow was then inspected by a corporal and its condition recorded. We were then marched off to acquire bedding and were issued with, blankets-five, sheets-two, pillow cases-two, and a newly laundered mattress cover. We were also issued with green one-piece boiler suit overalls, referred to as 'denims'. These we would wear most of the time, particularly for all weapons and combat training activities.

This hut seemed to be even older and more basic than those at either Aldergrove or Cardington. In the centre of the room, about two bed-spaces from either end were round and narrow black iron stoves with chimney pipes leading up into the roof. By each stove was a steel rectangular box-like bunker, also burnished black. These were full of coke. One of the bunkers was just opposite my allocated bed-space. I noticed it had the words 'Good luck you poor bastards' chalked in large letters on the side facing me.

The Ablutions were in a separate wooden building and I could foresee, as it got colder it would mean a chilly walk in the mornings and on any night calls. The greatcoat, I would soon discover, also served as a very necessary dressing gown!

Back by our beds we were given instruction on making bed-packs, by the corporal IC hut, having introduced himself as Cpl Martin and informed us that he was a DI. Here, the bed-packs had to be made up of a much higher standard that than we had done previously. The demonstration pack made up by Cpl Martin looked like a slice of fancy layer cake cut with a very sharp knife. Each blanket and sheet folded precisely and layered, blanket, sheet, blanket, sheet, blanket, with the forth blanket, wrapped and tucked neatly and tightly around the stack. So tight and neat it looked like a coating of marzipan on the layer cake! The blue stripes that ran down the centre and full length of RAF issue sheets had also to be lined up and centred precisely. The fifth blanket, an under-blanket, was stretched drum-skin tight over the mattress.

We had several practice goes ourselves and at each attempt, good or bad, Cpl Martin showed his contempt for our efforts by pulling off the under-blanket and scattering packs in all directions! I was proud of my forth attempt, which I thought was pretty good. But Cpl Martin thought differently. Up in the air it went!

When our corporal tired of this game, or thought we had got the message, he stood us to attention by our beds and lectured us on hut cleaning and 'room jobs', making dire threats about what may happen if the hut came below standard. He emphasised that this hut was going to be the best in the Squadron. So, it seemed, we were now part of a Squadron?

He confirmed this with his next statement, "You in this hut belong to 18 Flight of 'C' Squadron and you are going to be the sharpest, smartest Flight on the Squadron. RIGHT?"

He obviously expected a response from us and but when none came he again bellowed, "RIGHT?"

"Right…" came a desultory response and he again bellowed, "RIGHT, WHAT?"

"RIGHT <u>CORPORAL</u>!" we chorused.

"THAT'S BETTER! AND REMEMBER... I'M ALWAYS RIGHT," was his response. He then reached in a pocket and brought out a fistful of green coloured plastic discs and walked the length of the room dealing out the discs. They were flung in the general direction of each bed-space but as they had the aerodynamics of a one-winged bird they went everywhere except where intended. As mine came towards me I made a grab and caught it in mid air. That was a mistake! No sooner had I caught it than the corporal was right in front of me, his face inches from mine. "WHO TOLD YOU TO MOVE?" he roared. I could tell what he had had for lunch! But I was not the only one to try and 'field' the flying discs. The corporal bellowed, "STAND AT ATTENTION, MOVE ONLY WHEN I TELL YOU TO!" It appeared that we were supposed to suffer the indignity of crawling round on the floor looking for the discs.

Having been verbally chastised we were informed that the discs were to be placed behind our cap badges to identify us a belonging to 'C' Squadron. Having said that he asked, "HAS EVERYBODY GOT ONE".

"YES CORPOLAL," we chorused, but one lone little voice piped up, "No corporal," to which the corporal responded, "WELL, SEARCH FOR IT! If you don't find it, see me later. Unfortunately, I live here with you." From that we learned that the corporal occupied the 'bunk' at on end of the hut, which would mean he would be on our backs twenty-four hours a day. On the other hand we would be up his nose round the clock as well.

The corporal next appointed a 'Senior Man'. It was a natural choice. He picked an older chap, quite elderly compared to the rest of us. From his display of medal ribbons he was obviously another re-enlistment. When the corporal asked his name I think he was sorry he did. The name was almost unpronounceable and sounded like 'Petjeronoff'. It was confirmed later that he was Polish. His first name was also unmanageable to English speakers, so we, and he, settled for 'Pete'. I was to discover that there were many more like Pete, Poles and Czechs. All had served during WWII but could not, or did not want to return home because of the Communist takeover of their countries. They had found it difficult to settle in civilian life so came back into the Service, where they were welcome. Some I spoke to had a genuine belief that there would be war with Russia. They wanted, once again, to 'do their bit' and free their countries as they had hoped for in World War II. But most of them had been out of the Service for several years so had to go through the whole process of 'Basic' and 'Trade' training all over again.

Having appointed a 'Senior Man' the first instruction to him was to march us off to tea. It was now that late. It was only a few hours since we arrived but it already seemed like a week!

Before leaving us in Pete's charge, Cpl Martin had a last parting shot or shock for us! "Full kit inspection first thing tomorrow, o-nine-hundred. Layout as on the notice board. And lay out your lockers too. Be sure you get it right". He then addressed Pete, "Senior Man, sort out the room jobs, hut inspection too." He then bellowed, "AT EASE", and then departed, leaving us in any state but at ease?

Here, as well as bed-packs we also had to lay out lockers. Shirts, underwear, PT kit, kitbag etc. had to be stacked and neatly squared off on the shelves of the bedside locker. The kitbag had to be squared of on a shelf of the small locker with our Service number and name showing. Webbing packs were squared off and neatly stacked on top of the tall locker. Clothes kept in the tall locker had to be hung in a prescribed order. The only private space we were allowed was the small drawer of the bedside locker!

Pete marched us off to tea in the prescribed manner. Our mug-n-irons in left hand, tucked behind the back, right arm swinging. As we were forming up, other squads marched by. From their standard of marching it was obvious they had well started their training. Marching with a swagger, arms swinging in perfect unison, the squad looking like a group of synchronised windmills! I wondered as to how long it had taken to reach that standard.

Our squad shambled along to tea as we now had many in the group who had never properly marched before. Even with Pete calling the cadence, "Eff-ta, Eff-ta Wyyt-ta, Eff-ta" was of little help, it just made matters worse. But we got there and back, still as a group!

After tea, when back in the hut, we had time to pause and get to know each other. There were four of the Irish Flight, including myself, in the hut. By chance we had been shepherded together when we got off the train and had remained together. We were now a mixed bunch, both National Service and Regulars. But we Regulars were referred to as 'Volunteers' and were in the minority, both in this hut and on the Squadron.

Many of our National Service hut-mates found it hard to understand why we should volunteer to serve. There were looks of disbelief, and sharp intakes of breath, when they learned that many of us had actually signed on for ten years! Most of those doing their National Service, it seemed, were reluctant conscripts and saw it as a serious disruption to their lives and careers.

A few of the NSAs on the Squadron were in their mid-twenties having had their National Service delayed or 'deferred', to use the correct term, until they completed studies or apprenticeships. Some were University graduates and were now AC2s with Degree qualifications. We had one very well educated and cultured chap on the Squadron. He was an archetypical academic whom we, naturally, called 'the Prof'.

Because of his very cultured manner and speech I thought he might be a target for the DIs and other staff. But it was not the case. He sailed through basic training, taking it all in his stride. They, perhaps, more intimidated by him, than he by them? I am sure it was his manner of speech, most definitely of the officer class.

On this first evening, after getting acquainted, all thoughts, and conversation, turned to more immediate problems. Having to prepare for kit inspection first thing the following morning. A group formed round the notice board to study the kit and locker layouts. It looked simple, but to the unpractised, not at all simple. We had discovered that at Cardington. But there it was only a check that we had everything. Here we were in 'Bullshit Land,' as somebody remarked. Pete suggested we try a practice run.

Most of us did so. It was easy enough to place the items of kit according to the layout photograph but getting it to look exactly like the photograph was another matter. Our efforts looked more like a stall at a Jumble Sale. Even the experienced Pete did no better, and remarked, "No time to do dis bullshitt duringkt de voor". We gave up, packed our kit away and decided to leave it until the morning. We were here to learn, was the general opinion. So let our teachers teach!

Pete then decided to allocate the room jobs. There were lists on a clipboard on the notice board with the jobs pre-printed. He first tried democratic means, saying, "Pick your own jops". That was a disaster as everyone wanted to do 'Floor' (polishing) and Surrounds', the easiest jobs on the list! The 'Surrounds' job just involved picking up litter around the outside of the hut. However, as the dropping of litter carried a penalty worse than death 'Surrounds' would always be an easy job.

'Ablutions', 'Stoves' and 'Windows' (outside) were the most unpopular jobs for obvious reasons. 'NCOs Room' (the Bunk) was also a very unpopular room job as it put you very much in the direct line of fire from the corporal. Therefore our 'Senior Man' had to abandon democracy and adopt autocracy. But in the interest of efficiency and fairness that's how it had to be. But with twenty in the hut sharing the tasks it would not be too arduous. The tasks would be rotated over the six weeks of our stay, which seemed a fair enough system. A fair system even if I did land the 'Ablutions' job in this first instant as I had at Aldergrove.

As 'Reveille' was at o-six-thirty we were sure we would have time to complete the room jobs and have the kit layout completed in time for inspection at oh-nine-hundred

Morning came with the 'tannoy' blasting out 'Reveille' and in this instance all were out of bed in short order and making for the ablutions. And so it was with the other huts that shared the facility. With not enough washbasins to cope with this number all at once, we had to queue. With so many wet shaving it took some time. And here we could not go to breakfast in 'dribs and drabs'. We had to stay together and march as a squad.

While waiting my turn to wash and shave I had time to notice that variety of razors in use, many using the open or 'cut-throat' type. Some were using the patent 'Rolls' razor, which was a semi-safety model with a blade that could be re-sharpened, using a special 'strop', incorporated into its case. I, and most others used the 'bog-standard' safety razors.

No electric razors, but one of the lads in the hut had a novel clockwork model. But he needed to wind it several times to get a full shave. My razor was bit of an antique and heirloom. Made of solid brass and had been in the family since World War One.

By the time the whole hut had completed their ablutions and could muster, it was just after oh-seven-hundred and oh-nine-hundred was looking very close now. There was also a long queue in the dining hall, so it was an abbreviated scoff and quick, very quick, march back to the hut. It was just after oh-eight-hundred so less than an hour to inspection. Half an hour to get our room jobs done and the rest of the time spent in frantic kit layout.

A waste of effort as it turned out! Dead on the dot at o-nine-hundred, Cpl Martin, with another corporal we had not seen before now, arrived. Even before they entered in the room they were bellowing, "STAND BY YOUR BEDS".

On entering they just progressed down the room, taking a side each, pulling the blanket from under each layout! Having completed the destruction, one of them bellowed, "DO IT AGAIN AND DO IT RIGHT, THIS TIME". We did the layout again under their very close supervision most getting demolished, yet again.

Finally, when they were happy with our layouts or had decided that they were as good as they were going to get, they carried a minute inspection of every item in the layout. Everything was criticised, everything described as 'manky'. But this was our first day and all our kit was still in its 'as issued' state? It was Cpl Martin who inspected my layout, which he did with curled lip and disdainful expression.

My brass razor took his interest. "Brass, polish it" he remarked. My toothbrush then took his attention. It was new, of natural bristle and supposed to be slightly brown in colour. "What's this manky object, looks very unsavoury"? He held it up and regarded it as one would a dead rat! Then said, with a contemptuous sneer, "Then, its owner looks a not very savoury object. New one, by tomorrow". To argue I knew would be pointless, and very foolish, in the current circumstances. I would have to play the game and replace a perfectly new toothbrush?

Our lockers got the same treatment. The corporals tossed their contents out onto the floor and contemptuously nudged the items of kit into further disarray, with the toe of their boots.

Once they had completed their exercise in demolishing our characters and kit layouts they switched to the constructive mode and instructed us in brass, boot and shoe polishing. The boot and shoe polishing not just brush to shine but the good old military 'bull'. The old traditional 'spit and polish'. But not spit but tap water, in the lid of the polish tin.

By using a duster cloth and the index finger, the polish applied to the toecap of the boot in small blobs, with a small drop of water. By rubbing in small circles and repeating the application of polish and water it was possible to bring up a brilliant shine. But first it was necessary to smooth out the pimples on the new leather. This was achieved with the aid of the handle of the knife of our eating iron set. The pimples could be smoothed away by the application of polish and water and rubbing hard with the handle of the knife. It took time and was not achieved with the first try. We were given strict instructions not to 'burn' our boots or shoes.

That seemed like a daft statement but what was being referred to is a method of achieving a high gloss by applying a thick layer of polish and setting it alight. Extinguishing the flames, of course, before leather burned. The thus melted on polish could be burnished to a very high gloss.

A forbidden method because it was considered dangerous. The process could result in damage to Government property, be it just to footwear or at worst, a barrack hut burning down. But often a blind eye turned in the interest of an extra smart turnout. As I would learn, as I served longer, rules could be broken to achieve a good result but be prepared to suffer the consequences if caught.

We were informed that there was to be a further inspection the next morning and improvements were expected. When this very first session of instruction ended we were assembled outside and marched off.

Our destination, we discovered, was the Camp Barber Shop. There we were subjected to the regulation 'short back and sides' and had to pay one shilling and six pence (7.5p) for the privilege. I was already 'short back and sides' in style and had a good haircut the day before arriving in Belfast but that was now nearly two weeks ago. The cut here was very short, on the premise that no hair, at all, should show below the cap.

While waiting for my turn in the chair I saw some sad sights.

Being 1953 it was the time of the 'Teddy Boys' with their DA trademark hairstyles. Because of the styling, combed to resemble folded wings at the back of the head it was called the duck's arse of duck's anatomy, abbreviated to DA. Here was a line-up of carefully and expensively cultivated DAs awaiting the attention of the fiendishly grinning barbers. They were taking an obvious delight in this particular act of vandalism.

Many of these well cared for coiffures were already piling up on the floor. One lad was actually in tears as his pride and joy fell to the shears. Indeed, it reminded me very much sheep-shearing pen, with a fleece being peeled off every few minutes.

Our trip to the barbers was to be a weekly ritual. Sometimes, it could be even more often. To fall foul of a DI would often mean being sent for a haircut just for the hell of it! The barbers, of course, were quiet happy to take the 'one and six' and glide the clippers over our already well shorn scalps?

This first visit to the barbers took us right up to lunchtime. And no sooner back in the hut after lunch than a voice boomed out, "OUTSIDE, YOU LOT". It was a new voice, which we learned belonged to Cpl Wiltshire, who was to be our Flight DI for the duration of basic training. We got outside to find ourselves forming up with the occupants of adjacent huts. So combined, we formed 18 Flight.

Once formed up, we received instruction in basic drill movements from Cpl Wiltshire. He was assisted by another corporal who's name I cannot remember. We were drilled in Flight sizing, using the 'right dress' drill and forming three ranks from two.

It started in shambles, as expected, but improved with each attempt. The rapid progress, no doubt, due to the thunderous bellowing and withering remarks from the DIs. Parentage, gender and our membership of the human race, all being but in doubt.

Once our DIs seemed happy that we had a rudimentary grasp of these basic drill movements we were marched off. Or shambled off as marching together was to be our next lesson.

Once we started 'marching' it was odd to see so many who had been walking normally all their lives suddenly lost their sense of coordination? Arms now started moving in unison with legs? Right leg forward with right arm forward, left leg forward with left arm forward!

But the next couple of hours sorted that out as we covered miles up and down a back road of the camp, learning our left foot from our right foot. Most in the Flight got the hang of it quiet quickly as many seemed to have been associated with organisations that did some form of marching, albeit the Scouts, Boys Brigade or just at school. But still there were those who could not start off on the left foot and keep the pace, thus bringing down the wrath of the DIs on all of us. As case of one wrong, all wrong! Up and down we marched, the DIs bellowing out the pace, loud and clear, "EEFT - EEFT, YYIET, EEFT," (Left – left, right, left.) This first drill session lasted all afternoon, right up to teatime.

As well as our DIs calling the pace while marching, timing was also called in drill movements, at least in the early stages. First the DIs called the timing, "ONE, PAUSE, TWO, PAUSE" etc. Then we had to take up the call, and do so, until the timing became instinctive.

After tea, on this first day, it was straight down to the 'bull' and preparation for the next morning's inspection. We had now also acquired 'Blanco' to clean our webbing. The 'Blanco' was an RAF blue-grey coloured paste. Applied evenly with a brush to the webbing it gave it a fresh and new appearance.

It was very useful for covering up the metal polish stains that occurred from cleaning the brass buckles and tabs. Webbing belts were to be worn, on all occasions, except in the dining hall, from now on. That piece of kit was subjected to constant and close inspection so needed our special care and attention.

Our 'bull' session lasted right up to 'lights out'. Fortunately the lights stay on in the ablutions so we were able to wash and shower before turning in. It was very quiet in the hut that second night. Some quiet conversation but none of the banter of our first night. All very tired and some, I am sure, suffering from mild shock. It had been a very long day and the kind of day that very few of us had ever experienced before.

~ Chapter X ~

The first week of 'square-bashing' seemed very hard and I had to remind myself that it would only last for another five weeks. But the shock tactics worked and things got better as the 'breaking down' phase slowly turned to 'building up'.

We got used to the hustle and hassle and the quick changes from full uniform to physical training (PT) kit, or denims, depending on the next activity, and back again in the impossibly short times allowed. As we got back to the hut after one activity the call was always, "OUTSIDE IN FIVE MINUTES IN (No. 2, PT kit etc.), MOVE!"

Strangely, as we became more proficient in drill and other activities many of us seemed to get some enjoyment out of our basic training? That was never admitted openly by anyone but it was evident from a general cheerfulness that grew in the Flight. The gloom and doom of the first week was soon replaced by camaraderie and the glimmerings of 'esprit de corps' as our DIs fostered competition with other Flights. Being called, "YOU ORRIBLE SHOWER" became less frequent and this taken as a mark of our improvement.

There was genuine satisfaction and sense of achievement in doing things right and earning grudging approval from the DIs. We were lucky in having Cpl Wiltshire as our main DI. He was, no doubt, good at his job, very firm but very fair. Our Flight made rapid progress under his guidance and instruction.

In the second week, having become just competent in foot drill, we were issued with rifles. These were the Lee-Enfield Type 4, 303-calibre bolt action, with the long snout. I had handled the short Lee-Enfield, the standard British army rifle of WWI and still in use in WWII. In the 1950s it was still in use by the Irish Forces. My familiarity was the subject of some joking. Because I was Irish, there were suggestions that I had probably handled guns since infancy.

That was, in fact, close to the truth. Having being brought up in the countryside I became familiar with shotguns and sporting rifles from a very early age. Also my father was involved with the local defence forces during the war so firearms, including the short Lee-Enfield rifle, became familiar objects to me.

With the rifle, we were issued a webbing sling and a bayonet, the bayonet a 'pig sticker' type with its black metal tapered tubular scabbard. We had, of course, to sign for these items and told to memorise the rifle serial and butt numbers, as only the rifle issued to us would be accepted back. We were also told, in no uncertain terms, that to lose or cause malicious damage to a rifle would mean our automatic Court Martial. This was no empty threat, as it appeared that rifles did go missing. It appeared that there was a market for firearms and there were those who would pay a tempting sum for any such weapon.

Rifles were never shoulder slung and the sling was never used as a sling, it was purely for appearance and to add a bit of swank to rifle drill. It produced a nice sharp crack sound when slapped in the final movement of the 'present arms'. And, of course, it was yet another item of webbing and brass for us to 'bull'?

Bayonets were also for purely ceremonial purposes, although we did do some charging about and engaged in frenzied stabbing of straw filled sacks. But mostly we just polished them, drilled and paraded with then on our rifles.

Drill with bayonets fixed was always conducted with the Flight in 'Open Order'. That was for ceremonial purposes but was also a good safety measure. The added distance between ranks of the open order would just about put the centre and rear ranks out of range of flying bayonets. Although we had ample practice and drill in fixing bayonets there were those who remained cack-handed at that simple task. It was not uncommon for the odd, not properly fixed bayonet, to detach and become airborne, during rifle drill!

Of course we had the old cliché as featured in many war films and books. Always refer to a rifle as a 'rifle' or a 'weapon' but never as a 'gun'. However, our particular rifles could be used only for drill purposes, having come to the end of their useful life as weapons. On no account were they to be fired using live ammunition. They were certified only for use with blank rounds. But regardless of their deprecated state we could still suffer fate worse than death for loss or damage.

However, they still served a useful purpose. We drilled with them, stripped them, cleaned them and named the parts. Fired blanks during combat training. Which got them really dirty and the barrel fouled and so needed the maximum effort in getting them clean and back to parade standard. Every morning parade started with the 'port arms for inspection' and if the bore did not gleam like a mirror, from breech to muzzle, wrath descended!

Even though we inspected our own rifles and gave the bore a last pull-through before going on parade, specks of dirt would somehow to be there for the DIs to find. We held the opinion that there were spiders and small insects in the pay of the DIs, to crawl into rifle barrels and cause us grief.

Those rifles were our constant companions and bedmates. When not in use, kept slung under our beds, secured to the bed-frame by the trigger guard, using our personal 'D' rings and padlocks.

The 'D' rings were not the only bits of essential equipment we had to supply at our own expense! The baths and sinks in the ablutions were without plugs! We had to buy our own, from the NAAFI, of course. They stocked a 'universal' plug suitable for sink and bath. It was a flat flexible rubber disk that stayed in place by the pressure of the water. These plugs were an essential part of our toilet kit and were to remain so for many years of my service. Rarely did I see billet ablutions that had sink and bath plugs already in place. I had to reach the rank of sergeant to gain that privilege!

The ablution cleaning room job would often entail unblocking sinks or baths that had been plugged with toilet paper! The paper was government issued. In fact it had the words 'Government Property' printed on every sheet, top and bottom, in the best British Civil Service tradition, It was as rough as sand-paper and almost completely waterproof, so did form an effective sink-plug!

So precious were our personal bathplugs that I had seen many keep them on neck-chains like identity tags! It was a standing joke that in the event of a disaster where individuals could not be identified, at least it could be determined as to which were definitely British servicemen. They would be the remains found with neck-chains with the remnants of bathplugs attached! But such security measures were not without good reason! Often, in the hut, on mornings, some victim of petty theft would be enquiring, "Wot rotten sod as' nicked me bathplug?"

The NSAs were not particularly pleased at having to acquire such necessary items at their own expense. Having to buy bathplugs was bad enough but also having to purchase 'D' rings and locks to secure their rifles, was a source of much moaning. As they were paid such a pittance, less than half the Regular rate, I suppose they had good cause to resent the imposition.

Having to purchase cleaning materials mostly for the purpose of 'bull' was also cause for moaning among the NSAs. And some Regulars too! When cash was short and the choice was between fags or Blanco, it had to be the Blanco. Although such items could be shared, each individual had still to have the full range of cleaning materials displayed on kit layouts. Even the containers for those commercial items had to be 'bulled'!

Metal polish and cleaning cloths were issued for hut cleaning, of brass window fittings and doorknobs etc. But woe betides anyone caught making personal use of those materials.

Our weapons training included the 303 rifle, Bren light machine gun (LMG) and the Mills hand grenade. We were also introduced to the Sten submachine gun (SMG). Training to shoot concentrated on the rifle with considerable live firing, culminating in a test. Ten rounds applied (in our own time) and ten rounds rapid (as fast as you can but try and hit the target).

I did well, getting an inch group on the applied and all on target and in the prescribed area of the target, in the rapid fire. The instructor remarked that I had qualified for 'Marksman' but it could not be officially awarded on this twenty-five yard training range. In shooting, I had an advantage of previous experience but my competence brought on yet more jokes concerning the Irish connection?

We fired at figure targets, life-size plywood representations of charging enemy solders. At twenty-five yards it was impossible to miss, but at that range all shots had to be grouped within set limits, to be considered good shooting.

For safety, the range was within a high brick walled enclosure and the targets placed in front of a sloping bank of sand with a high wall behind that. I noticed that there were bullet holes high up on that wall! Considering that firing was from a prone position those stray shots must have been off target at an elevation of at least fifty degrees? Very few on our Flight proved to be that bad at shooting by many did completely miss the target. Causing the instructor to remark that some would do better to fix bayonet and charge!

We did have one trainee who put a couple of shots high up on the rear wall, to the despair of the instructor. He was heard to remark, "I think you put one over the top. You'll have to go and apologise to the farmer, you may have shot one of his cows!"

But many had never, until this time, handled a firearm, never mind fire a rifle as powerful as the 303. It had the reputation of a powerful recoil 'kick', which could cause bruising or, at worst, break a collar-bone. Lurid stories, second-hand and exaggerated, were told in the barrack-hut, that reinforced the bad reputation of the 303. It was, therefore, not surprising that some first shots completely missed the target. It is difficult to hit anything, with a nervous tremble and eyes tight shut. The 303 had a powerful bark but seldom bit its handler. And properly handled it was tame to the user, but deadly to the enemy. We also had lectures on basic ballistics and the trajectory of the 303 – the trajectory being curved due to the effect of gravity and air resistance, etc. Our instructor illustrated the trajectory by chalking a line on the blackboard, showing the shallow rise in the early part of the projectile's flight and sharp decent to ground at the end. At the end of the lecture he asked if we had any questions. Brian, a hut-mate, and one of the Irish Flight, had this question.

"Does it mean that if you lay the rifle on its side it will shoot round corners?" It was an old joke and instructor rose to the occasion, "I said that the round fell because of gravity, the pull of the Earth. If it weren't for that every time you fired, if you stood in the same spot long enough you would shoot yourself up the arse... and in your case, Paddy, that would be fatal, seeing as it's where you keep your brains!"

Training with the Bren LMG was mainly in handling, disassembling, reassembling, cleaning and finally firing – each of us firing some single shots and a few short bursts on automatic fire.

We only had demonstrations of the firing of the Sten SMG. But did learn to strip, clean and reassemble it. But not even a demonstration of the grenade. Too dangerous, we were told. There had been fatal accidents in the past so even demonstrations were discontinued.

Even on the demonstrations, grenades had failed to detonate and armourers were put at risk making 'duds' safe. We were told that the grenade was an indiscriminate offensive weapon and would never be used in the purely defensive role we would be required to play during our service. However, it had not been phased out of recruit training and still included in the weapons training programme?

We trained with dummy grenades. Using the then standard 'Mills Bomb' the familiar 'pineapple' grenade that had been in use since WWI. We practised fusing and setting the striker etc. And doing that without losing an eye! The striker spring could propel the striker a full ten yards if the trigger lever was released with the base not screwed in place! In demonstrating this danger our instructor released a striker without the base in place. The flying striker should have safely bounced off a wall but shattered a classroom windowpane! We got the message but wondered if we trainees would have to cough up for 'barrack damages' of the broken window?

What I did learn about grenades dispelled the myth of the film heroes who pulled the pin with their teeth. If you did not have dentures before attempting that you stunt might need a set after the event. As for that other cliché so often seen in films, triggering then counting before throwing. Considering the standard fuse had a four second duration, such a stunt might surely result in an own goal! A seven second fuse had been used in the past and some of those had been 'returned to sender'.

The only grenade throwing we did was to practice lob the dummies in an open field. We up formed in two lines of a distance of just over thirty yards apart, a good average throwing distance. One line would lob the grenades towards the other line. They were picked up and lobbed back.

However, some exceeded a thirty-yard throw, which resulted in ducking and weaving and an appreciation for steel helmets! Some of these heavy iron Easter eggs bounced on the hard ground and one or two were 'skittled' off to Sick Quarters for treatment of bumps and bruises.

All this combat style training was termed GDT (Ground Defence Training) was to enable us to guard and defend our stations and units against possible ground attack. All the instructors for this phase of our training were from the RAF Regiment and while in their charge we moved everywhere 'at the double'. Double time march is a brisk trot and a Flight at the double in hob-nailed boots sounded like a steam train as it progressed along the station roads.

GDT also involved an introduction to war gases, the various types and precautions, and some training in the use of respirators (gas masks). The effectiveness of the respirators demonstrated by entering a gas chamber filled with tear gas vapour.

We entered the chamber with the respirators on and took them off after a few minutes. We certainly noticed a difference without them. We were kept in the chamber longer that most could hold a breath. We exited coughing and with eyes streaming and taking at least half an hour to fully recover from the effects.

Before entering the chamber we were given strict instructions that once out to run and keep running to clear the gas from lungs and eyes. There was an overwhelming desire to rub the eyes but on no account were we to do so. That would only prolong the irritation.

We also had a demonstration of mustard gas and had a tiny drop, in a diluted form, we were told, dabbed on the backs of our hands. Soon most of us quickly developed a blister reminding us of its other name of 'blister gas'. As I mentioned in an earlier chapter, I had an uncle who had been gassed in WWI. Seeing the blister on the back of my hand I realised how he and others must have suffered, having breathed in the stuff!

We had some lessons on nuclear and biological warfare, mainly in the use of basic radiation detection and monitoring equipment. But this was very basic and we were given to understand that it was a complex subject and proper training left to special and specialist courses. It would be the 1960s before NBC (nuclear, biological and chemical) warfare was given really serious attention.

Our training, then, gave the impression that a nuclear strike would result in some large explosions, but was survivable. Our training would be needed in the aftermath to assist in decontamination and recovery.

Most of our training took place outdoors, and in all weathers, but quiet a fair amount of physical training taking place in the gymnasium. That was a very large and very well equipped establishment. We followed a directed program of rigorous physical exercises but were also encouraged to take part in various sports activities in the evenings and at weekends.

The emphasis was on team sports and anyone with ability or interest was co-opted to play for the Squadron in weekly matches. Those of us not selected for such teams were 'encouraged' to partake in indoor sports, such as five-aside football, badminton, fencing, weight training and boxing.

Also some martial arts, such as ju-jitsu and kendo, but only demonstrated. Trainees were not allowed to participate unless that they had proven previous experience. But there were those who claimed to be exponents of ju-jitsu, only to suffer the embarrassment of really expert PTIs, proving otherwise!

There was a lot of encouragement to get involved in boxing, as inter-Flight matches seemed to be a strong tradition. I was coerced into taking part and took a battering as a result. But my face on parade the next day brought respect from my peers and the DIs. But I was not alone. There were others with black eyes and bruises.

The protection of sparing helmets or gum-shields were not considered as necessary at that time. Not surprising then, that I, and a couple of the other boxing participants were required to see the MO (Medical Officer) and the Dental Officer.

I had been generally fit before I enlisted, skinny and wiry in build as a result of cycling, rowing and generally pursuing an active outdoor life. However, after a few weeks of RAF physical training I had become positively athletic. Many expressed surprise at gaining the ability to shin up a rope as if it was a ladder and being able to easily somersault over a vaulting horse. We did a lot of running as many PT sessions involved long runs. All this effort built up to a final six-mile cross-country run.

After the apprehension and despair felt in the first week of 'square-bashing' most now seemed to sailing through it. There were only two events that I regarded as black spots, one personal and another that affected the whole Squadron.

We were all very shocked by the suicide of one of our fellow trainees in the third week of training. One morning while in the ablutions, he cut his throat! Just quietly did it at the sink in the company of his hut-mates. No one realised what was happening until it was too late to prevent it and then all too shocked to give any real help, even if they could.

The rest of the Squadron only learned of the tragedy after morning parade. Most of his hut-mates had been absent from breakfast and from the parade. Those who did attend seemed unusually subdued and there were rumours of a serious incident. After that morning parade we were marched to the gymnasium, which was unusual since we were still in No. 2 dress and had our rifles.

When assembled there the Flight Commander informed us that there had been a 'tragic incident'. We were told that whatever we knew of the matter we were not to discuss it, even among ourselves. There were hints of dire consequences for anyone who communicated anything concerning the incident to 'outside agencies'. It was not to be mentioned in letters home!

But in spite of the threats the matter was discussed. Some of his hut-mates spoke of it. It was revealed that it was not the pressure of training that drove him to such terrible action, but a very personal problem. But out of respect I will not disclose further. I do not remember if he had a military funeral, as we were not involved. Our training continued, and the incident was never mentioned again.

There are those who find the pressure of training hard to bear. They have taken the harsh treatment as personal and feel that they are being bullied and have resorted to self-harm as a result. But such incidents seemed rare, or at least we did not learn of many.

As for bullying, I never experienced such. Harsh treatment, yes, but our DIs and instructors were very even handed. No one was ever singled out, we all got equal 'stick'!

As well as physical fitness we also had numerous lectures and lessons from medical staff on personal hygiene and in keeping generally healthy. Great emphasis was placed on prevention of VD (venereal disease). That part of our training was certainly designed to scare the crap out of us.

We were shown colour film of infected organs and treatments were described. The treatments all seemed worse that the disease. Especially the instrument known as the 'umbrella' used in the treatment of gonorrhoea! The application of this treatment shown in close up graphic detail! We all have heard the story that our grandfathers had bromide put in their tea to dampen ardour! We had colour films!

The message seemed to be that all casual sex would guarantee a 'dose', but if we must indulge then use a rubber and visit the ET (early treatment) Room as soon as possible, after the event.

All military units, in those days, had ET Rooms equipped with anti-infection kits. The ET Rooms were normally attached to the Guardroom so in a very public place. The door to the ET Room was clearly indicated by a red light above it. All that and the prospect of the self-administered treatment were very off-putting.

Application of the ET had been part of our anti VD training. It involved the insertion of the long snout on a small tube of a powerful antiseptic ointment and squeezing the contents into penile urethra!

The lurid content of these lessons was surely to put us completely off sex. These particular lessons and lectures were delivered early in our training programme. The aim, no doubt, was to curb our carnal instincts, at least for the duration of our basic training?

Another treatment that was almost a bad as the disease were the mandatory inoculations against tetanus and typhoid. More commonly known as the TABT jab. We had this in an open air mass inoculation session. We queued in two lines and receiver the 'jab' form teams of medical staff working at two tables. A separate medical team for each line, left and right.

As I was in the process of receiving my jab at the right-hand table, the bloke on my immediate left collapsed in a faint! It seemed that seeing all those needles going into arms ahead of him was too much to take. I did not blame him and I had avoided looking. They were using bloody big needles that must have hurt, judging by the wincing and expletives from many of the recipients.

The collapse of our wilting hero caused a few moments confusion while the body was removed. It that confusion I ended up in the left-hand line and received yet another jab! The medical orderlies could not remember giving me a jab, nor believe me in stating that I had already been jabbed? The red weald left by the needle on my right arm was not accepted as evidence. They maintained that I had probably pinched myself to make it look as if I had received the jab? However, they gave me the benefit of the doubt and I received the second jab in the left arm!

All very amusing for my fellow trainees, but quickly forgotten as another little drama started to unfold! One trainee was completely panicked by prospect of the needle. He broke ranks and crawled under a nearby hut.

The MO and several NCOs were trying to persuade him to come out. A little 'good guy, bad guy' act ensued with MO gently cajoling while the NCOs bellowed dire threats of pain and grief far worse than any needle. Whether it was the gentle persuasion or threats that decided him, I do not know, but he eventually came out, had his jab and was marched off under close arrest.

Immediately after the jabs session we had rifle drill! The theory being that the arm exercise would help disperse the serum into our systems and reduce any soreness and stiffening in the injected arm. In my case, both arms!

That may have worked for some but for me the next morning told a different story. I woke early with a fever and arms like balloons. It seemed I had a bad reaction to the TABT jab. So had a few others in the hut but at least they had only one arm affected.

Soon after reveille, Cpl Martin bounced into the room, He yelled out 'ANY SICK', but his look and tone said 'there better not be any sick'! It appeared that casualties to the TABT jab were expected. But I and the other victims stayed silent! We were not going to give that little shit the satisfaction and an excuse to sneer.

We took all kinds of flak from the DIs, and other instructors, but it was part of the training game and never personal. But our Cpl IC hut seemed to take a delight in the personal insult. I often wondered if his attitude was also part of the game? He seemed to target the Regulars and we Irish in particular. We thought he might be deliberately trying to provoke and weed out any of us who might be considered 'temperamentally unsuitable for service'? He certainly did push his luck but we resisted the provocation.

We started with rifle drill that morning and seeing that many had been affected by the TABT jabs most thought this a bit sadistic. But such exercise was thought to be the best remedy for our stiff and sore arms? It was not surprising that many, and myself in particular, took a lot of stick for a below par and ragged performance.

The weeks went by and we, as individuals, and the Flight as whole, improved out of all recognition. The shambling herd of only short weeks ago now worked as one. We were now all functioning as synchronised parts in a marching and drilling machine. Our DIs also showed a change in attitude and became more relaxed as we shaped up to their expectations.

We were by now also totally obedient and acting only on the word of command. Doing nothing, not a blink, until told to and when told to, acting immediately! Our conditioning well illustrated one morning while marching.

The Flight was marching along a back road of the station and as we came to a junction in the road we expected the command, 'Right (or) Left Wheel'. But our DI was busy remonstrating with some unfortunate towards the back of the Flight, so the command never came! So on we marched, straight ahead, through a ditch and into an unfenced ploughed field, like Lemmings over a cliff!

What our DI had to say I will leave to the imagination? It appears that there are times when we were allowed to use initiative, and that instance was one of them. We regretted that lack of initiative as we laboured long to get our muddied boots back to standard.

In the forth week the Flight had to supply a number of people for sentry duty on the main gate. We had now reached the standard that had so impressed me the day I arrived, and first saw the sentries. I was short-listed for that duty and went through the drill. But only the tallest and smartest six were picked and I was not among those.

It was also in the forth week that I had my personal black spot, a heavy interview with the Flight Commander. That at the behest of the MO!

As we arrived back at the hut after a session on the assault course I was instructed to report to Sick Quarters. I was to go immediately, but no reason given? I hastily changed into No 2 without taking the obligatory shower and hurried off to Sick Quarters, wondering what it was all about. On arriving at Sick Quarters I was ushered into an examination room, told to strip to the waist and wait. I complied and very soon the MO appeared.

He took one look at me and exclaimed, "You're filthy, airman. How dare you report in that state"? I then realised I was streaked in mud from the assault course. I tried to explain but made matters worse by admitting I had not showered before reporting. I got a swift lecture on personal hygiene and informed that the matter would be reported to my Flight Commander.

The MO then got on with the real reason for my reporting. I needed to have a colour vision test! It appeared that the cursory test in Belfast had found me to be deficient in colour vision? Perfect colour vision being deemed essential for the trade of Radar Operator, so I now needed to undergo a more rigorous test.

On this new test I was shown a lot more Ishihara Test charts and the MO remarked that there was nothing wrong with my colour perception, perfect for the trade of Radar Operator. When I answered his question as to where I had the pervious test, he muttered, "Incompetent shower"!

I was then dismissed but the MO again reminded me that my flight Commander would be hearing from him. I left Sick quarters wondering why I had to strip to the waist for an eye test and was now in trouble as a result! That evening Cpl Martin gleefully informed me that I was to report to Flight Office the next morning, immediately after parade.

I duly reported the next morning and was marched into The Flight Commander's office. The Flight Commander, a pilot-officer, who looked not much older than myself, lectured me as if I had committed some heinous crime and had brought the Squadron into serious disrepute! He pointed out that should I come to his attention again in like manner I would be 're-flighted'.

That was the ultimate sanction during basis training. The ignominy of having to join a more junior Flight and repeat a week or two of training was indeed a dire threat. Leaving me with that thought I was dismissed. But my actual offence, my 'filthy state', the real reason for me being carpeted, was never mentioned?

My next transgression soon followed. Fortunately a minor sin, and did not require the attention of the Flight Commander. My room job had been stove cleaning and a cigarette packet was found in the stove on the morning inspection. That was to the seeming delight of Cpl Martin. But he was aware that I did not smoke, and to give him his due, he did ask for the real culprit to own up. No one did so I had to take the blame and as punishment I was to clean both of the hut and the NCOs room stoves for a whole week.

It was October and as the stoves were burning at night, cleaning had become a hard and dirty task. All of the coke ash had to be cleaned out to the last speck and then the stove completely black-leaded, including chimney pipe. Cleaning a single stove in time available was bad enough so I despaired of being able to manage three before o-nine-hundred each morning. But my hut-mates were very sympathetic and the wise and experienced Pete, our Senior Man did not see fit to change the room job routine. Having not been told otherwise he continued to allocate two people to each stove so the only task I had to do alone was NCOs room stove. God bless Pete.

The cold nights showed up the limitations of our heating system. With both stoves well stoked with coke and going full blast they did warm the room to reasonable level. But keeping that level of warmth quickly exhausted the fuel. There was never enough fuel to last the full week at the rate we needed to use it. We, therefore, tried to solve the shortage by mounting occasional night raids on the Coke Compound.

It was easy to gain access to the compound. It was enclosed by a low brick wall and topped by a chain link wire fence. Entry could be easily gained by unfastening the bottom of wire from the supporting metal stakes. It was easier than many of the obstacles on the assault course! A fire-bucket full of coke could fuel two stoves for most of an evening.

The coke raiding parties from different huts acted independently as each thought that the idea was solely their own. Consequently, there were delays and some missions aborted as parties dodged each other, thinking the other were the Security Patrol.

I know of no of instance of anyone being caught and brought to book for thieving coke. I even had the thought that our short ration of fuel was due to a knowledge that it would probably be made up through our own enterprise anyway.

At least no one was ever caught and reported by the Security Patrol, as that was comprised of our own. Every trainee had to perform that duty at least once during training. The Patrol maintained an all night vigil on the station and the emphases was on being at a named checkpoints at given time.

This schedule was rigorously enforced with an NCO doing random checks to see that we maintained the timetable. This system made illicit movement very easy as once the patrol was past a particular point it would not be there again for a known period of time. This made the coke raids very easy.

When we went out on patrol we were issued with a truncheon, a hand torch and a whistle and a Patrol Card listing the reporting points and times. We were given a briefing on the patrol schedule and told to strictly adhere to the card. The use of the torch was obvious but there was never a mention of circumstances in which we should use the whistle or truncheon?

If ever it was too cold to stay in the hut there were diversions and attractions to take us out for a few hours, bull permitting. There was the NAAFI and the cinema or trips into town. The latter only allowed in the final weeks when it was considered we were of a high enough standard to be allowed out in uniform.

As already mentioned, the gymnasium could be used in the evenings. There was the boxing, also mentioned. That was an opportunity for trainees to legally take a swipe at members of staff. But there was a risk and price to pay in challenging staff. There were some good boxers among PTIs and members of the RAF Regiment and they did not spare trainees for their foolishness. Fortunately, I never came up against staff. It took just a fellow trainee to see me off.

A Forces Show was held in the gymnasium one evening, which the whole of RAF Bridgnorth seemed to have attended. The star of the show was Dick Emery, then famous on radio and later became very popular on television. The gymnasium was packed with men in uniform, reminding me of forces concerts I had seen in films. To get a good view of the stage there were blokes sitting up in the rafters and up high on the horizontal bars that lined the walls of the gym. Many old familiar wartime jokes and songs got an airing but were received with thunderous laughter and tumultuous applause.

We also had a Squadron concert arranged in the NAAFI in our final week. Attendance was optional so I, and a few hut-mates decided to go to Bridgenorth town for the evening. On a pervious visit to a popular café in the town we had got talking to some girls and now hoped to meet up with them again.

Cafes with their jukeboxes were a common meeting place for teenagers at that time. But the girls were not there on that particular night so we found a pub. The lads with me had ale and expecting that I would only drink that well known national Irish brew so one of them bought me a pint. Not a favourite of mine, but national pride was at stake so I drank the stuff! But we were just one-pint wonders and with that single drink downed we returned to camp.

We were back in the hut by twenty-two thirty and soon the concertgoers returned, just before 'lights out'. We were told of the great evening we had missed and the great talent had emerged from among our Squadron members. It appeared the there were some good musicians and budding comedians among us who made a great contribution to a very entertaining evening.

We countered their chides by lying about the great 'talent' we had met in town. But we were immediately shot down when someone remarked, "If the talent was that great how come you managed to tear yourselves away and be back so soon, more than a whole hour before you needed to be?"

At the end of square-bashing we would have two weeks leave and travel warrants to take us home. For me, that was very good value as my family were in the West of Ireland.

Unlike those from mainland UK and Northern Ireland, we from the Irish Republic could not travel home in uniform. Our civilian clothes had been sent home but now the RAF would provide us with 'civvies'. We were measured up and the suits duly arrived in our final few days of training.

Trying these on was a hilarious affair. Even the stern faced corporals who had delivered the suits could not resist laughing. The styles and colours ranged from city gent to bookie's clerk and very few fitted. I was lucky in receiving a half decent brown number but the trousers were about two inches short in the legs.

I found that if I wore my braces loose I could make up the length and hoped I would not to trip over the crotch! Others tried to get better fits by exchanging jackets and trousers, but as there was not a single style or colour the same. Also, the suits had to be signed for so what was issued had to be returned. The suits had arrived bundled up and tied tightly by stout cord they were in need a good deal of brushing, sponging and pressing to get then into wearable order.

All kinds of stories came out as to the origins of the suits. From being taken off unidentified copses to having being donated by the condemned. Another suggestion was that they could be rejected demob suits. Pete said that this was a possibility as he had been issued with a demob suit on leaving the Service. He said he had been given a choice. It was a limited choice, but had managed to get a suit decent enough to get married in.

In the final week of our basic training all effort was going into preparation for our Passing Out Parade. We were being subjected to very detailed inspections on morning parades and most of day the whole Squadron was on the square rehearsing the full parade, complete with band playing. We spent hours practicing the Review Order march past and getting the whole Squadron synchronised in foot and rifle drill. Ever since that week whenever I see the Guards on the Trooping of the Colour I can understand why even they sometimes have a wobble in their lines.

But all my practice and rehearsal was in vein, as I did not attend the Passing Out Parade! It seemed that medical matters have priority over even this, the most important event in our basic training!

During the weeks of training we all had routine dental inspections and it was decided that I needed treatment and had been given a number of appointments. Like many, I am averse to dentists and was pleased to find that my final appointment was on the morning of the Passing Out Parade.

That dental appointment I would surely not have to attend? Our passing out Parade must be considered far more important than a dental treatment? But that was not the case! The RAF actually considered medical matters to be very important. The Dental Officer had priority. So while the Squadron drilled on the parade square I had to suffer the dental drill.

I arrived back at the hut to see the final moments of the parade. I could view a large part of the square from one of the hut windows. But I was not the only one to miss the parade? Brian, one of my Irish hut-mates, had blown himself up the evening before and had to go sick with a hurt hand! I had to share the blame for that? Guy Fawkes night was close at hand and we Irish were indulging in the novelty of fireworks. Their sale banned the Republic some years before as the result of a horrific accident. But they were on sale in the NAAFI and some big kids, myself among them, had bought some. These were mainly used to play childish tricks on each other, such as rolling them under doors of occupied toilet cubicles, and bathroom, etc. Mostly the fireworks used in this manner were non-exploding spectacular types that just emitted coloured flames and sparks.

But the odd 'banger' was also used! On the evening before our final day Brian came hurrying from the ablution block and asked me if I had any fireworks. It appeared that someone on who Brian needed to get revenge was now ensconced in the toilets. I had a box of assorted fireworks on my locker top and Brian grabbed a few and made off back to the ablutions.

There soon followed a bang of an exploding firework so I assumed Brian had evened the score, but I though a 'banger' in a toilet was a bit much. Moments later Brian came back into the hut, clutching one hand, his face was screwed up in agony. The pillock! He had lit the fuse but not realising it was a 'banger' and held too long! Two of the fingers of his right hand were lacerated in the explosion! We took him to Sick Quarters to have it attended to. As well as dressing his hand we got a sound, and well deserved, dressing down by a member of the medical staff. Brian was very upset at his stupidity and I felt responsible by having provided the firework. He could not handle a rifle so was off the Passing Out Parade but that was no consolation for his very painful hand.

Those of us travelling to the Irish Republic had to crate all items of kit except one shirt, a tie, socks and our shoes. The wooden crate lid had to have painted on our Service number, name and address of the trade training station to which we had been assigned. The crates were well used so we also had to first paint out the details of the previous user. Once packed and secured they would be taken to station Stores for forwarding to our new unit. That would be the very next morning when we would don our RAF issue civvies and pack our No 1 blues.

Soon all my other hut-mates were back in from the parade and very relieved that it was all over with. The parade was the final seal that marked the completion of our basic training.

The rest of our last day was spent in tiding up, cleaning and returning rifles, and other items such as the green denims on loan for the duration of training. Contrary to lore, we were not allowed to mess up the hut to make more work for our successors. Instead we did have to give it a final clean. The only concession was our not having to clean the stoves the next morning.

Many of the NSAs left that afternoon but those of us travelling further afield had to wait until the next day. And on that last evening we had a farewell party with our Flight DIs invited. That was held in a pub in Bridgenorth town. They brought their wives or girlfriends so we could see that they really had a human side, after all. But with square-bashing now behind us, all could be forgiven.

In the relaxed atmosphere of the party we did learn a couple of 'trade secrets'. How the staff berets were such a neat fit and how their 'blues' seemed to be lighter in colour and of a smoother material that our hairy outfits. The smaller crown and neatness of the berets was achieved by shrinking. By the process of plunging the beret alternatively into hot and cold water the crown would shrink by a considerable amount! As for the lighter and smoother 'blues'? The smoother look was achieved by literally shaving the woolly nap off the fabric. The lighter shade of colour came about naturally after a few dry cleaning treatments!

The shaving process needed great care and was strictly forbidden but the 'blind eye rule' applied to beret shrinking. In the interest of ultra smartness, training staff had an unwritten dispensation to use any means to set a good example and achieve that extra smartness.

I had to admit, that the training staff did have a difficult job to do and they did it well. We were now finished and off on two weeks leave. They would be starting with a whole new 'orrible shower' after the weekend!

And I must say at this point, that in spite of the frustration and provocation we caused them our DIs seldom resorted to bad language! The strongest terms or expressions they used to chastise us were never worse than 'orrible shower' or 'orrible little man'. The worst that could happen was to be accused of being 'idle'. With our RAF Regiment instructors the odd 'F' word would slip out. But that in conversation, and never directed at any individual!

An example of that occurred during our very first classroom lesson on the Mills grenade. The RAF Regiment sergeant instructor opened the lesson by producing a grenade from below the lectern. He pulled the pin, fumbled and dropped it and yelled, "OH SHIT, TAKE COVER"! and threw himself flat on the floor.

He was very surprised when none of us moved? On getting to his feet he exclaimed, "What's the matter with you lot. Too shit-scared to move? You could all be dead by now!"

It was our University graduate, the Prof, who spoke up. In his best Oxford accent he said, "Actually, sergeant, we did not think that a man of your experience could be so clumsy as to drop a live grenade". The sergeant was taken aback, but retorted, "Oh actually! Actually, I think you buggers are all too effing clever."

The fact was that we had forewarning of that particular sergeant's party piece from members of a senior Flight. We had anticipated his dramatic opening to the lesson.

The morning of departure, immediately after breakfast, we returned our bedding, changed into civvies and packed the last of our kit to send to Stores. That final morning, the few of us left shared the room jobs that still had to done.

The others were very surprised when I volunteered to clean the stove in Cpl Martin's bunk and set the fire for lighting that evening! After cleaning and resetting, in order that the fire would get going well, and quickly, I laced the kindling with fireworks! Our Cpl Martin could start his evening with a bang, or few!

~ Chapter XI ~

About mid-morning of the departure day, we long distance travellers were trucked to Bridgenorth railway station. From there started our journey home, by the prescribed shortest and cheapest route. First, by rail to Holyhead, and then by ship to the port of Dun Laoghaire, near Dublin. We looked an odd bunch in our assorted civvy suits, but all in RAF blue shirts, black ties and black and very shiny RAF shoes. We looked like a party of mourners on the way to a funeral!

It was now late October, cold and damp and we were without overcoats. Those of us feeling the cold were wearing our RAF issue lightweight pullovers under our shirts. The only luggage we carried were small cases or haversacks, containing just our toilet things and a change of underwear.

We had a group of Welsh lads from the Squadron travelling with us on their way home. They put us right with regard to the stations and train changes we would have to make to get to Holyhead. One of these lads remarked that when we crossed the Menai Strait to look out for the station with longest name in the British Isles, if not the world. He pronounced the name of the station. It started with 'Llanfair', then lots of Welsh tongue-twisting whistles and squeaks and ending in 'gogogouch'. The full name is *Llanfairpwillgwyngyllgogerchwyrndrobwlldysiliogogogoch*, shortened to 'Llanfairpwll' for non-Welsh speakers and no doubt for economy in printing and sign writing mostly seen on maps today as simply 'Llanfair PG'. We looked out for it and did see it as we passed through. It could hardly be missed as the sign ran nearly half the length of the platform. Seeing that firsthand, a place name that was so often featured in quizzes and poor jokes, would mean little to today's well-travelled youth. But for most of us in 1953, who needed to join the Forces to see any of the world, it equated to seeing the pyramids of Egypt today!

One of our gang discovered he could pronounce the name and decided to show off. He kept on repeating it until we were irritated into threatening to throw him off the train!

We all supposed that Holyhead was on the isle of Anglesey, but one of our group was taking bets that it was not? That was our linguistic smart-arse! It started a friendly argument but none were so sure as to actually put money on their convictions. The challenger was, of course, right, Holyhead is on a small island off Alglesey, called Holy Island!

We arrived early in Holyhead, hours before the ship was due to leave. As I remember, not due to sail until around about midnight. We spent a boring hour or so in the bleak embarking shed but then decided to explore nearby small town of Holyhead.

By then it was getting on for 10 pm and all seemed closed for the night but we found a small café that was still open. There were about ten of us and we filled the place and were made very welcome. It was the most customers they had all week and had to make fresh sandwiches to satisfy our needs. They had been about to close but stayed open on our account.

But they did closed at 10.30 pm and we were left to wander the deserted streets again. It was as quiet as the grave and even house lights were very few. As we noisily ambled down the main street a policeman approached us. In a fine Welsh accent he addressed us, "Good evening boys and what might you be doing out at this time of night?" We explained we were waiting to board the Irish ferry. He went on, "Well keep it quiet boys. You'll be making people nervous and they'll be calling me on the telephone". We apologised and informed him that we were on our way back to the quay but would now proceed more quietly.

We boarded the ferry for a very rough overnight crossing. It was a very old and un-stabilised ship that heaved and rolled like a drunken sow in any kind of rough sea and that particular night it was rough in the extreme. I am fortunate in that I do not suffer from seasickness but with many others around me being sick and with the resulting state of the toilets, awash in it, I did get a little queasy.

There were frequent and lengthy calls being made to Hughie on the big white telephones, on that crossing!

It was an early morning, and very welcome arrival at Dun Laoghaire. But even on the rock solid quay the sensation of the heaving deck remained, and did for many hours after. There were many pale and washed out faces in the crowd awaiting the train on the quay platform.

A short train journey into the city of Dublin and then it was the parting of the ways for the Irish contingent. However, most of us would be returning from leave on the same day and by the same route, so would meet up again. Two of us were to train at RAF Yatesbury and several others close to there, at RAF Compton Basset. Most of the group were from Dublin or close to the city, but ahead of me was a long, all day journey back to County Clare in the West of Ireland!

The first part of that journey was without changes, from Dublin to Limerick, and then a local train to Ennis, County Clare. From there it was just a few miles more to where my parents lived. But getting there from Bridgenorth had involved a full two days travelling.

As I was waiting for my train to leave Dublin, I decided to send a telegram to my parents to confirm my time of arrival. I then boarded my waiting train with still time to spare.

Just as it was about to depart an American serviceman came tumbling in, just it the nick of time. He asked if this was the Limerick train and I confirmed that it was. He took the seat opposite me. He was a young chap, about my age, and although in an American army uniform he sounded very Irish. I was curious and got talking and asked him how he came to be serving in the US Army.

It turned out that he had a lot of relatives in America and had stayed with some of them on prolonged visit. While in the States he discovered that being Irish and having American citizens to act as sponsors, he could enlist. He had just completed all his training and had been posted to Germany. He was now on leave and visiting relatives in Limerick.

~ Chips for Breakfast ~

He was an Infantry machine-gunner and had 'buddied up', as he put it, at the end of training and now his whole machine-gun crew were in Germany. It seems that in the US Infantry, a group of friends can team up and stay together on posting! I envied his very smart uniform and rate of pay but sure I did not want his job.

There was another small group in uniform on the train. In very smart uniforms and I thought that they too, were American. Then I saw that one had an Irish Army rank of corporal insignia on his sleeve. But the Irish Army uniform in those days I knew to be not that smart? I soon realised that these very smart uniforms, much smarter that the RAF, were, in fact, of the Irish Air Corps! But I still really thought that I had made the best choice. I would see much more of the world that I ever would see in the Irish Air Corps.

I finally arrived in the small town of Ennis and completed the last few miles by taxi. The taxi driver asked if he call in at the Post Office as he had something to pick up and deliver out on the way I was going.

When he came out of the Post Office he was smiling. As he got back into the drivers seat he said, "Very handy, you can deliver this", and handed me an envelope. It was the telegram I had sent that morning, from Dublin!

Although I had been away for just a couple of months it was the longest period I had ever been away from home. So it was to a great welcome and happy to be back if only for a short stay. And I had money to spend. With my latest pay, savings and credits I had nearly £20, the most I ever had in my pocket!

But the money and my leave was soon spent and the day to depart for RAF Yatesbury, wherever that was, soon arrived. My return travel warrant was for a place named Calne near Chippenham, in Wiltshire. I managed to locate it on a map.

For the return I took an early morning train from Ennis and met up with the others, as expected, on the quay at Dun Laoghaire. Brain, my hut-mate, did not join us and had not appeared before we sailed? I hoped his absence was not due to his damaged hand as I really felt I was part to blame for his injury. But one of the others said that he was in two minds about returning and had said that before the mishap with the firework. He had been given a very limited choice of trades and had been persuaded to train as a Cook?

Unlike our homecoming journey, the return crossing to Holyhead was over a calm sea. Also not many onboard so we managed to stretch out on the bench seats and get some sleep. Also plenty of space on the train to Crewe and managed some kip on that leg as well. We took turns so we had someone to wake us in case we missed our change. At Crewe we went our different ways, only four of us travelling on together. I was never to meet any of the others after that night except the one chap who also trained at Yatesbury and another at Compton Bassett. The RAF of the 1950s was a very large organisation and could easily swallow up individuals. Friendships so formed were nearly always temporary.

Our now much diminished group eventually arrived at Chippenham and then on by local train to Calne. A very local train as it just shuttled between Chippenham and Calne. That was before Dr Beeching had wielded his axe. During my time at Yatesbury I would often travel to and from Chippenhan by that train. We called it the 'Chippenham Flyer' but fly it did not! It was so slow it could be caught even after it left the station.

One night a group of us actually caught the last train back to Calne by running after it down the track. This would often mean travelling in the guards van but the Guard seemed used to and accepted this situation. His occasional, but unsolicited, fee was a few cigarettes or of bottle of beer. Ah, how the world has changed! If the last train was missed we walked along the track, the shortest route back to Calne.

That little train always stopped at a place called Black Dog Halt. That stop seemed to be the middle of nowhere, open farmland all around and not a dwelling in sight. In all the journeys I made I had never saw anyone get on or off the train as that stop? A group of us were on the train on one occasion, bound for Chippenham and bemoaning the slow journey. Overhearing our complaining another passenger, a local gentleman, remarked, "Tis fine in late Summer, though, you can lean out the winda and pick blackberries"!

On this very first journey I made, the train was almost full of RAF personnel returning to, or like me, joining training courses. Trucks were waiting at Calne station to transport us to RAF Yatesbury or Compton Basset. It was late afternoon when we finally arrived at RAF Yatesbury

It turned out that I had arrived days before my course started so spent a few days in a transit hut. I was the only one of the Irish group joining a Radar Operator course. The other Irish chap, David McMahon, was joining a Radio Mechanics course. The next morning the two of us went to Station Stores to collect our kit. Mine had not arrived! I had actually started the training and had spent the first week the course in civvies, before my kit did arrive.

As I had arrived early I was put to work in the Training HQ helping with the course joining procedures of other trainees. I had problems with my own official arrival as being in civvies I was treated with some suspicion. That was compounded by the fact my documents had not arrived so there was no prior notice of my arrival. Fortunately I had my F1250 ID card and a valid Form 295 (leave pass).

I was placed in care and charge of Sgt Barrel, a stocky gent who resembled his name. But a good boss during what was my first small, but real, contribution to the workings of the RAF. I had expected a sergeant to be proportionally fiercer than a corporal. Not so with Sgt Barrel. He was firm, fair and good-humoured, with a bark a lot worse than his bite.

When my fellow course members had assembled I moved from transit accommodation to the Course hut in 'Y' lines. It was the usual black wooden building accommodating twenty, except that here there was central heating of sorts. The radiators comprised a pair of large-bore pipes set against the walls either side of the room. Not very efficient at emitting heat, but then the hot water had to travel nearly a quarter of a mile from the boiler house through badly lagged pipes.

I soon got to know my course-mates. As wide a mix as there had been in the hut at Bridgenorth, and again the majority were NSAs?

Which begged the question? I, and the other Regulars had to enlist for ten years to enter the trade of Radar Operator, yet NSAs with only two years to serve, had been given that trade? When I queried the point I got the same spiel as I had at Trade Selection! Ten year Regulars were needed to form the backbone of the trade, the future NCOs? The NSAs, serving only for two years, could fill only junior posts? But some were serving for three years. Those conscripted for National Service were given the option of serving an additional year to gain the Regular rate of pay. These three-year Regulars seemed to be mainly married men and some that had been unemployed. All of my course-mates, except the few like me, on long-term service, were aghast at the idea of serving for ten years.

My course-mates were, again, an interesting bunch, from all walks of life and wide experience for such young lives. But some were not so young. There were a couple who had seen WWII service. Occupying the bed-space on my immediate left was a Polish chap in his forties. He had served in the RAF through most of WWII as a cook but had only reached the rank of SAC. He had medal ribbons for war service and some I did not recognise, from other service. His name was Sidorchsky but we called him 'Sid'.

It turned out that he had actually been a colonel in the Polish army and had been taken prisoner by the Russians. As a prisoner he had been used as a slave labourer in the forests of Northern Russia. He told me of the terrible time he had and almost did not survive the Winter there. Men and horses froze to death. But dead men meant more clothing and dead horses, a good meal! Providing, of course, their Russian overseers did not take it all for themselves.

However, when Russia joined the Allies against Germany he came to Britain with hundreds of other Polish servicemen. In spite of his rank of colonel he had very little real military experience. His post in the Polish army had been as a Director of Music. He had been in charge of army male voice choirs. When he came to Britain he spoke no English and had no documentation or any proof of his army service or status. All that was offered him was general service in the RAF and so he ended up as a cook.

The war had ended before he actually did get hold of his Polish army records. Other members of his family had also come to England and had set up business in Manchester, running a fish and chip shop. On leaving the Service at the end of the war he worked in the family business. When his English improved he decided to give the RAF another go. All he was offered, this time round, was again a trade in the ranks. And so he was now training as a Radar Operator.

He made many friends on the Course, me included. But he was very much a father figure and we all had great respect for him. His spoken English was good but he did have a very pronounced accent. He still had a very keen interest in music and tried to organise a choir from the Course members. But male-voice choirs are not a strong tradition in England, so there was little interest in that idea. Except, naturally, from a couple of Welsh lads among us. But a duo is a few short of a choir!

Sid's story was confirmed by another great character I will always remember. That was Cpl Ryder, our NCO IC hut. He was another WWII veteran, with an aircrew brevet, and the Pathfinders insignia, and a fine row on medal ribbons including the DFM! (Distinctive Flying Medal) He had flown on Lancasters and had held the rank of Warrant Officer. He was another father figure to us. He was firm in his supervision but never raised his voice and got everything he wanted from us through the natural respect we had for this veteran airman.

He had continued to serve on after the war ended, but as Bomber Command contracted he could no longer continue on flying duties. He managed to retain his rank of Warrant Officer but had to take a ground job in catering. He was not happy as a catering officer and was trying hard to get back to flying. There were vacancies for crewing new types of aircraft but he was considered too old for conversion training.

He bitterness came to a head during a Commanding Officers inspection of the Airmen's Mess he managed. It appears he had an altercation with the CO during which the CO's hat was filled with fried eggs and chips! And that, I was told, was how Warrant Officer Ryder DFM, became Cpl Ryder!

We learned that, not from him, but from one of our Course instructors. It is a great story and I am sure it is true. I was to meet a lot like Cpl Ryder

RAF Yatesbury was the usual big sprawling hutted station, utility built to meet temporary wartime needs and still in use well beyond its expected life. One perimeter fence ran parallel to the A4 and on the hillside beyond, carved out in the chalk, was the famous Wiltshire White Horse. It could be clearly seen from most parts of the station. It was tinged with colour and was red, white and blue, when I first saw it. The RAF Boy Entrants had applied that patriotic colour scheme. It had often suffered in such a manner, having the occasional paint job or alterations to its anatomy. Seen, on occasions, as a stallion of impressive proportions.

The Boy Entrants had just finished at Yatesbury by the time I arrived. But only just, as their mark could still be seen, and not just on the White Horse. There was a barrack hut bent in the middle to form a shallow 'V'.

As a parting gesture one Flight of Boys decided to saw a barrack hut in half! They had managed to saw completely through the all wooden structure, roof, walls and floor. And then they knocked selected props from under it so that it bent in the middle. That incident, I believe, generated a record sized defaulters parade. The whole Squadron were put on 'jankers' (punishment parades, three times a day)!

The results of another of the Boy's escapades could just be seen on the roof of the station cinema. The manager of the Astra and the Boys were not the best of friends. He had them banned from the cinema on several occasions for rowdy behaviour. The then manager was a heuristically challenged individual and suffered teasing on this point by the Boys. It was quiet a serious matter to be denied such a main source of entertainment in their young lives so they took revenge. During one night they painted on the cinema roof, in very large letters that could be seen for miles, the words,

'Baldy's Bughouse'! This was quickly painted over but remained just discernable for years after.

When my Course got under way I soon discovered that that there was more to the radar operating trade than I imagined. It turned out that I was to train as a Radar Operator PPI (Plan Position Indicator). The PPI being the standard radar display that traced out the responses from rotating radar on a cathode ray tube (CRT).

By overlaying a map reference grid on the face of CRT, radar responses, such as those from aircraft or other objects, would be displayed in their actual geographic location. I had assumed that my job would be to operate the display equipment and report the contacts to a control centre.

But that was only part of the job! The UK Radar Control and Reporting (C & R) system, I discovered was a very large and complex organisation and radar observing just a small but very important part of it. At that time the system that had evolved during WWII was, more or less, still in place but big improvements in radars and support equipment were coming in. In the meantime we were training on some of the equipment and most of the methods that had played a part in winning the Battle of Britain.

The training was carried out at the Air and Ground Radio and Radar School (AGRRS) or 'Agress' as it was more commonly referred to. It was on a separate site just a very short distance from the main station. We paraded each morning outside the huts and were marched to the site via a concrete pathway across open fields. We marched to and from lunch and back each evening in all weathers.

Our corporal instructors were in charge of this process but it was not the strictly disciplined marching of square-bashing. They would remain to the rear of the Flight, in a gaggle and talking among themselves. One would occasionally remonstrate and call out the pace if we began to lose step but mostly we were left like an old dray horse to plod along on our own. We would often test their vigilance by seeing how far we could extend the Flight before they noticed. The leading file would increase their stride and widen the gap between them and the next file and the process would be repeated through the Flight until it was extended to about three times its proper length! This did not please our instructors and we would suffer a few days of strictly controlled marching. But after that few days they would relax and we would start the game all over again.

I found the course interesting but there were also many tedious elements. The most interesting was, of course, the actual radar operating. The setting up and operating the radar display consoles. Most of the training was conducted in small rooms referred to as Radar Cabins. The cabins simulated the live conditions, with blacked-out windows and very dim lighting.

I was very impressed when I entered a cabin for the very first time. The eerie glow of the radar displays, the high-pitched whine of electronic equipment and that particular aroma of hot electrical components. It was mysterious and exiting, until I learned more and got used to it.

Our initial radar training was mostly done on a large radar display console known as the R3202. This was the control and display console that had been used with the wartime CHL (Chain Home Low) radars.

The R3202 comprised of a PPI, a height finding display and all the associated control knobs, switches and dials. It was a piece of equipment that had seen better days and, no doubt, suffered under the awkward hands of countless trainees like myself. It tended to be a bit unstable and difficult to calibrate. But in being so it succeeded as a training instrument as it needed a skilled and delicate touch to set it up accurately and operate.

The associated height finding system was very basic, but could be acceptably accurate if used by a skilled operator. The height of an aircraft detected by the radar was computed by comparing the strength of the radar echo signals from a number of beams. The radar aerial, in the receive mode, was designed to form several discrete overlapping beams in the vertical plane. This system was a feature of many of the older metric wavelength radars and first used with the WWII CH (Chain Home) radars. This system was called,

'Split beam, signal comparison height finding', but simply referred to as 'Split Heights' by the operators.

The radar signals we received on the R3202 were, of course, not live from actual radar. A simulator, of just slightly lesser vintage but equal crankiness to the R3202, generated the echo signals we saw on the displays. The simulator was no electronic marvel, but a large black cabinet affair that generated the moving aircraft echo signals by a series of motor driven cogs and cams acting on potentiometers.

I think it was known as the Radar Simulator Type 21? It sat in room next to the R3202 consoles and whistled and cheeped like a hatchery of day old chicks. Occasionally the noises stopped and so did all our aircraft echoes, as the simulator stalled.

That would send our instructor scuttling to the simulator console where he would proceed to kick, body-slam and swear in an effort to resuscitate it. That worked most of the time but on occasions the expertise of a radar mechanic was called for. He would kick, body-slam and swear at it. That failing he would open panels and twiddle about and it would start working again. If the mechanic failed to fix it a fitter would be called. He would consult with the instructor and mechanic offer a prognosis and the mechanic would then fix it.

That was my first experience of the technical hierarchy that existed in the Service. When the equipment goes wrong, the operator knows *how* to kick it, the mechanic *where* to kick it, but the real technician, the fitter, knew *why* to kick it!

The R3202 simulated a low-resolution metric radar display on which the responses appeared like small bananas. To gain experience of the newer centimetric wavelength radars with more resolved responses, we were trained on consoles known as a DU5s (Display Unit Type 5).

The DU5s were set up in pairs, one as a PPI and the other as a height indicator display. In this instance the height was obtained from a vertical scanning (nodding) narrow beamed radar that enabled an acceptably accurate height to read direct from a scaled display. The DU5s were designed to work with the Type 14 plan position radar and the Type 13 vertical scanning (nodding) height-finding radar. However, the training displays were simulated.

The setting up and calibration of the DU5 involved opening panels and manipulating internal controls set close to lethal voltages. This brought some risk of electric shock but we were well trained in the necessary precautions. We avoided such accidents but did have a couple of examples of the DU5's ability to bite the unwary.

One morning soon after we started training, the console we were using developed a fault and a mechanic was called for. It appeared that the EHT (Extra High Tension) power unit, located in the base of the console, had failed.

The mechanic arrived, removed the unit's covering panel and poked about inside. There was a loud crack and a blinding flash and the mechanic vanished! When our eyes recovered from the flash we found him? His head, arms and legs were sticking out of the partition wall at the back of the cabin!

The force of the shock had propelled him to the back of the cabin with such force that his backside had penetrated the fibreboard partition wall. He, fortunately, suffered no serious injury but was taken to Sick Quarters for a check-up. Lucky, as it appeared he had come into contact with sixteen thousand volts!

As Winter deepened it got quiet cold in the training cabins. The consoles gave out a considerable amount of heat, especially from the EHT power unit of the DU5s. The covering panel would get quiet warm and provide comfort for cold feet. Which led to a young WRAF getting bitten!

She was on fire watch while the cabin equipment was being serviced. She was found by one of the servicing crew, unconscious on the cabin floor. She had received a severe electric shock but fortunately lived to tell the tale

It happened thus. It was cold so she had decided to warm her feet on the DU5 EHT unit cover panel. To get full benefit of the warmth she removed her shoes and placed her feet where the cover panel should have been? But the panel had been removed during the servicing so her unshod feet came in contact with a high voltage terminal!

And so another story was added to those our instructors would tell. They would relate such horror stories as object lessons in the need for great care in the proximity of high voltages.

But in spite of these safety lessons and cautionary tales we would still be tempted to play silly games with dangerous equipment.

There was an old metric wavelength radar on the site, used mainly for fitter and mechanic training but also as an example of 'live' radar for operator training. The transmitter and receiver of this equipment was housed is a hut and connected to the radar antenna via 'feeder lines'. These lines comprised of pair of parallel bare copper wires, similar to an old fashioned telephone line, running close to ground, between the equipment hut and the antenna. Because of the precise engineering and physics involved these bare wires carried the high frequency radar signals, but did not radiate them.

Trainee fitters and mechanics would use the open feeder lines to estimate the radar's wavelength by gauging what is known as the 'standing wave'. Running a metal object, normally a screwdriver with an insulated handle, along a feeder line would produce an electrical spark. The distance between zero and maximum spark was exactly half the wavelength.

The spark could also be produced with bare fingers and although a very low current ran in the lines the method was discouraged. But, of course, we had to try it! In our break time, when unsupervised, many did try this trick. The spark just tickled so seemed harmless enough. However, some did later developed sore and swollen fingers. And no wonder, their fingers had been cooked a method not yet available to the public. Although exposed to longer wavelengths in this instance, the effect had been the same. Their fingers had been microwaved!

As well as radar operating, there were practical lessons in other tasks associated with the trade. A lot of time was spent in practicing DR (Dead Reckoning) Navigation and Conversions.

DR navigation was carried out using a piece of apparatus known as the Craig Computer. Not electronic but a purely mechanical device that enabled the plotted track of an aircraft on scaled map representing the Ground Speed to be converted to True Air Speed. Its purpose was to assess the speed of target aircraft to aid their interception by fighter aircraft. But the most useful task in DR navigation was to assess 'Pigeons to Base'. 'Pigeons' being the distance and bearing of a fighter under control from its current geographic position to its home airfield.

In combat, a pilot could quickly lose his bearing and the ground based DR navigation could get him re-orientated. And very important, in the event of an air emergency, provide heading and distance to the nearest airfield.

'Conversions' was simply converting the range and bearing of an aircraft radar echo to a geographic grid reference to produce the familiar plots on a plotting table. The 'conversion' process was needed because some current radar, especially mobile and airborne equipments, did not always have map reference grid displays. A simple task, but the requirement was speed and accuracy.

Most of these skills were brought together in the performance of what were termed 'Crew Duties'. The typical basic radar reporting crew consisted or the PPI Observer, the Height Operator and the Continuity Plotter. The tasks of a PPI Observer, and a Height Operator have been explained. The job of the Continuity Plotter, as the job title implies, was to maintain a continuity 'plot' of aircraft detected and reported to him by the PPI Observer.

The crewmembers communicated with each other by telephone headsets, each with their part to play in maintaining the 'plot' of air activity in a defined area, swept by the radar. The PPI Observer reported grid position and direction on each aircraft detected, the Height Operator computed and reported heights. The Continuity Plotter maintained continuous plot of the movement of the aircraft reported. Using a Chinagraph (grease-pencil) he traced the movements, with directional arrows, on a back-lit gridded map. He also allocated an identifying number to each track, and recorded its height.

The Observer could report at a rate of four plots per minute, the rotational rate of the radar, but the Plotter had to maintain a 'plot' on at least twenty aircraft. The crew followed a strict 'track telling' procedure, an example as follows is for a newly detected aircraft: 'NEW TRACK - SOUTH WEST - CHARLIE HOW TWO ONE FIFE ZERO (grid position), HEIGHT ONE FIFE, TRACK ONE NINER'.

Training under simulated conditions was relatively easy, but there was a very strict observance of procedures. The Plotter had the most difficult job, made more difficult in training as we had to change crew positions about every ten to fifteen minutes. In that situation it was not easy to maintain continuity of tracking and often we would literally 'lose the plot' and chaos would ensue for several minutes. It was not surprising that the bulk of course time was devoted to 'Crew Duties'

Sadly, it was 'Crew Duties' that ended our Polish course-mate Sid's chances of becoming a Radar Operator. His accent was so pronounced that very few could understand him over the telling lines. He was dropped from the course and decided to opt for 'civvy-street' instead of another RAF trade. We had a little party to mark his leaving. He had decided to go back and work in the family business. We all received an invitation to free fish and chips if ever we visited his 'chippies' in Manchester.

For the most part, I enjoyed the course but despaired at times of reaching the levels of ability required. We were pressured and over trained to a degree of skill and accuracy that was above and beyond what would be required in the 'live' situation. But I would discover that only later, on an operational unit.

The most difficult part of the course were the associated 'theory' elements, as it involved the committing to memory of vast amounts of information. A large proportion of the information had little relevance to our practical tasks but was to be included in the end of course qualifying examination.

I could see good reason to know about all the duties I would perform and why I had to perform these tasks. But why did I have to learn, in full detail, the duties of all those in the chain of command, right up to the Commander in Chief? Why did I have to learn detailed technical specifications of radars, even those I may never see and some that had already gone out of service? All this superfluous information was indeed needed for the written test but served little other real purpose otherwise. Later I was to discover there were things that would have been useful to know, but this information was not included?

It was many years later before the knowledge element of training was to become fully relevant to practical tasks performed. In the 1970s the RAF adapted a systematic approach to course design and I was involved in that process.

However, most of the practical skills I acquired on the course were very relevant. Most of those basic trade skills continued to be used up until the advent of an ADP (Automatic Data Processing) based air defence system. That came into being in the early 1970s.

But the teaching method in the 1950s used to impart the 'theory' was extremely tedious and boring. Delivery was mainly by dictation, directly from manuals and textbooks. Very little use was made of training aids or devices to help in remembering. On my course, it was Sgt Lord who delivered the lectures and lessons, on most occasions.

Lord by name, but also lordly in his manner and speech. In his grand plummy voice he droned on from behind the lectern like vicar giving a sermon. He read aloud the text of our trade bible, from the tome known as C & R Procedure Instructions.

We did take notes, as everything had to be written down in the Stationary Office notebooks supplied. However, as most of the information we recorded was classified, the notebooks had to be surrendered and secured at end of lessons. Therefore we had no opportunity to study in our own time.

We tried to overcome our lack of further study by having verbal question and answer sessions back in the hut. But most wanted to relax in the evening and forget the tedium of training. We had heard of trainees who had risked smuggling out their notebooks and had even taken them home. We had learned of this from promulgated details of Courts Martial that had taken place as a result of notebooks being left on trains, etc!

Most of the classified information that may have been disclosed and resulting in Courts Martial is now freely available on the Internet. Not just information on equipment and systems of the 1950s, but very current information!

Our training in the 1950s put us in possession of classified information we did not really need to know, at least not until we were on operational duties. A lot of time and expense could have been avoided with application of a little commonsense. Careers were cut short and, for some, time spent in prison, all for the lack of that common sense.

But in the military situation such transgressions had to disciplined. Culprits brought to task for breaking Service regulations and failing to comply with orders, rather than breaching the Official Secrets Act, and revealing information useful to an enemy.

The course progressed and we did improve in skills and knowledge by following a relentless routine. A very welcome relief in our training day were the canteen beaks. But even they could be a bit farcical as far as we trainees were concerned. The AGRRS had one canteen that served all. Staff, including corporals and below, and trainees. Senior NCOs and officers, it seemed, had their own 'tea swindles'. The canteen opened for twenty minutes only, mid morning and afternoon.

But all the corporals other permanent staff were allowed to jump the queue, so very few trainees ever got served in the short time allowed. If I rightly remember, I was served only twice in whole duration of my training. It got to the stage where I would volunteer for cabin fire watch rather than take part in the pointless queuing in the canteen. It helped that I had not yet gotten much of a tea or coffee habit. That would come later when on operational duties, with long boring watches and little activity.

The lack of the means of further study in the evenings gave us the freedom to enjoy the social amenities on or off RAF Yatesbury. There were many. The Astra cinema, afore mentioned, with a programme change twice a week. There was the NAAFI with its bar, with various bar games, and the restaurant. There was always someone who could play the piano and singsongs would often ensue. We would gather around the piano in scenes reminiscent of the war years. Most of the songs too, were from the past. Other than the NAAFI there was the YMCA and Malcolm Club.

We would seek off-camp entertainment, most weekends. Groups of us would venture into the village of Calne, or further afield to Chippenham. Chippenhan was popular destination on Saturday evenings. The attraction there, were dances at the NAAFI Club. Not that I, or any of my mates were any great shakes at dancing. But the NAAFI Club dance was a big draw to the local girls. As all females had to be accompanied to gain admission, there were always gaggles of girls hanging round the entrance looking for lads to book them in. Often we would be conned into booking girls in, but once in they would stick with their mates and ignore us for the rest of the evening.

But not always, and dance partners for the evening could be found. But as I have said, I was not much of a dancer but didn't need to be, as dancing to 'Swing' did not require much grace and style in movement. Besides, the dance floor was always so packed it was a case of hold tight to your partner and go with the crowd!

In that close contact dancing and the crowded conditions I learned the hard way that it was always necessary for your partner to know where your hands were. Often, so called mates, dancing close by, would sidle up and surreptitiously lay hands on your partner in 'off limits' places! However, as that happened with such predictable monotony, most of the girls were wise to it.

The club bar was completely separate from the dance hall and drinks were strictly not allowed in there. Consequently the bar was crowded with the lads and most of the girls in the dance hall. The girls, dancing together or with the few brave lads that did not require the fortifying provided by the bar.

As mentioned, the girls should have been all accompanied, but they nearly always outnumbered the lads. That came about because the incoming lads would book girls in, have a beer, look the place over, but then move on, hopefully, to greener pastures. I was guilty of that on a few occasions.

But most of our spare time was spent on camp, which provided a good social life and we shared our evening time between the cinema, the NAAFI, the YMCA or the Malcolm Club

Although it did not have a bar, the YMCA was still very popular. It was a very good place to just socialise over soft drinks and tea or coffee. It also had the best range of indoor games, including darts, bar billiards, table tennis, chess and dominoes. In fact it had all the popular bar and board games and, of course, cards. I, and many other course-mates would often attend the YMCA and play the various games. To obtain sports equipment or games we had to surrender a personal item as assurance, normally our berets.

The YMCA building was not the most decorous of places. In fact it was drab and basic in its furnishings but it had the most friendly and welcoming atmosphere that I can ever remember. The club comprised of a single large room. In the centre of the room was a large black iron stove. It was always kept well stoked and a welcome source of heat on those very cold evenings. We would often just sit around that stove and chat.

It was in the YMCA club that I sampled my first ever packet of potato crisps. I had never tried them before and almost choked on the salt packet, the salt in those days, in a little twist of blue paper! I nearly swallowed it as I upended the crisp packet into my mouth, to get the last few crumbs!

Other than the NAAFI, the popular spot for a drink was the Malcolm Club. There the bar was a lot smaller but more pub-like than the NAAFI, and also very popular and nearly always crowded. It was also the preferred social gathering place for members of the WRAF and so very popular with the lads on that account.

I had my first physical encounter with a member of the WRAF at that Malcolm Club! A painful encounter as it happened. One evening a group of us were entering the club with me in the lead. As I was just about to enter the bar a WRAF lass bust out of the doorway. She bashed me round the head with her handbag and rushed on past and out of the main door, in tears!

As well as being hand-bagged, I was, of course, totally gob-smacked by the assault. My mates were also amazed by the attack but looks of surprise soon turned to leery grins. I tried to assure them that I had nothing to do with the poor girl's distress and nor had I ever seen her before. But they remained disbelieving, and even impressed. I was now branded a heartbreaker.

My reputation was further damaged, or enhanced, according how you wish to view it, by two other incidents. The first of these occurred as I was returning on my own from the cinema one evening. It was a very windy evening. As I walked towards my hut an object came bowling along the road carried towards me by the wind. The object was a hat, a WRAF No.1 dress hat!

I retrieved the hat and looked around for the owner who surely must be close by and looking for it. But not a soul in sight so I assumed it must have blown some distance. I decided to take it back to the hut and hand it in at the Guardroom in the morning. But as soon as I got into the hut the questions and suggestions came thick and fast. No way was I believed that I had just found it. Among the remarks were, "Come on, Paddy, if you persuaded her to part with her best hat what else did she part with" and, "What did you give her in exchange since you don't seem to have any kit missing".

There was a name on the label inside the hat and my first inclination was to personally seek out the owner. However, as it was a large hat size for a female and appeared to have seen some service, I decided to hand it in at the Guardroom.

The next incident occurred when I was on security patrol. A duty we had to perform during trade training as we did on basic training. As I was on my beat and passing the WRAF huts just after lights out, there was a commotion at one of the huts. Giggling, shrieking, and the sound of a door slamming. I went closer to the hut to investigate but a first saw nothing. I then saw movement in the shrubs by the hut. I called out, in the time-honoured fashion, "Who goes there". A female voice responded, "Make them let me in, I'm freezing" It was December, very cold and with a sprinkling of snow on the ground.

The lack of foliage on the shrubs did little to offer much in concealment. I could confirm that the person trying to hide was indeed female. That was not difficult to see, she being stark naked!

Being the gallant Boy Scout I took off my greatcoat, which she allowed me to drape around her. As I did so my hand touched her arm and I could feel goose bumps like cobblestones.

I heard giggling above me and saw faces at the hut window. I called out that I would have to involve the RAF police but the hut door opened and my, by now blue, damsel in distress was allowed back in. As the door slammed shut again I realised I was still without my greatcoat. I knocked and a hand soon appeared, offering the coat through the slightly ajar door. I donned my greatcoat but did not feel cold due to this warming experience!

I continued my patrol and on reporting back to the Guardroom, recorded 'NTR' (nothing to report) in the logbook. The naked WRAF was obviously a prank among friends, but on a night that cold she could have caught pneumonia. Chucking hut-mates out naked into the cold seemed to be some form of ritual for the WRAF and nudity in the shrubbery was apparently a regular occurrence. At least it added interest to boring night patrols.

A few days after my encounter, I, with my usual group of course-mates, paid an evening visit to the Malcolm Club. The bar was fairly full and quite a few members of the WRAF were in attendance. One group of girls kept looking in our direction and at me in particular. They were giggling among themselves so I discreetly checked to see if my flies were undone. They were secure, so I reckoned that, as they had been in the bar before us they must be the better of a few drinks. A short while later one of the girls came up to me and said, "Hello, don't you remember me?" I was surprised and completely miffed. Was it a case of mistaken identity and was I about to be hand-bagged again? But no. this girl was regarding me with a broad but cheeky smile. Seeing my puzzlement she then said, "Don't you recognise me in uniform?" The way she said it and with the particular emphasis on the word 'uniform' suddenly made me realise that she was my damsel in distress, or undress, as it was, of a few evenings ago. This was confirmed when one of her mates quipped, "He doesn't recognise you with your clothes on!" With that loud remark I became the centre of attention in the bar. The looks on the faces of my mates were a picture, with their chins on the floor! And now in proper lighting I could see my 'snow maiden' was not at all bad looking. I sincerely wished that I really was guilty of what was my mates were obviously thinking.

"How are the goose-bumps? You didn't catch pneumonia?" was all that I could say, but I could see that she was well insulated in the vulnerable area. She said she was fine and thanked me for the rescue and the loan of my greatcoat.

We joined the girls and it turned into a party, a farewell party, in fact, as it was the girl's last night at Yatesbury. So party we did that evening, and started new friendships. At closing time we escorted the girls back to their hut. It was a bitter cold night, so after a few moments of frozen kisses and cuddles with my new friend outside the their hut, we parted. But not before we exchanged addresses and promises to keep in touch.

But I never did write. When I found the note the next morning it was an illegible scrawl. It must have been the alcohol or the cold that caused such a wobbly hand. Certainly it was not passion. It was far too cold for that, and greatcoats and gloves are not conducive to arousal. The interlinking of the brass buttons of our greatcoats was the only coupling that took place. From the scrawled note I could just make out a name. And I had written both addresses? Ah well, June, what might have been? A trim little ship that passed in the night! A very cold night!

~ Chapter XII ~

In about the forth week of the course we had to move out of our hut in 'Y' lines, to allow for repair and redecoration. Our new and temporary home was a fairly dilapidated transit hut in 'W' lines. It was a case of 'take up thy bed and walk' having to move all kit and bedding ourselves. We were given the use of a couple of stores trolleys, small four wheeled flat carts, which was of some help.

Although billeted in 'W' lines we still had to use 'Y' lines Mess and NAAFI, so quiet a long walk to breakfast in the mornings. Also our working parade was still held on the 'Y' lines road. Dental hygiene took a back seat for most of in our hut while we stayed in 'W' lines. It was too far to go back after breakfast just to scrub up the pegs. I carried a brush and paste in a pocket but that idea ended when the paste tube ruptured in that pocket.

I only realised that when our instructor tapped me on the chest and said, "What bloody decoration is that then?" When the tube ruptured the paste had created a large white star pattern on my uniform breast pocket. It looked like the insignia of some 'Grand Order'!

The NAAFI temporarily lost our custom in the evenings while we were in 'W' lines as we now had the YMCA club only a very short and convenient distance away. Also we were now much nearer to the Malcolm Club. We spent more time than ever in those two establishments. Our first weekend spent in 'W' lines I will always remember.

That weekend was the birthday of on of my little group of pals so we celebrated the occasion in the Malcolm Club. Our little group had by now acquired a liking for stronger beverages. It being a special occasion we drank more than usual and our usual was not a lot, but some of my mates had a lot more than they were used to.

Our birthday boy and two others got literally paralytic! At closing time they got only yards from the club before falling in a heap. That left just two of us standing and he and I tried our best to get our rubber legged friends back to the hut.

We struggled along, more or less carrying them in a relay system. It was a struggle as we also not at our most sober. The birthday boy then flaked out altogether, leaving us; the most sober two, with three stiffs on our hands. So we, the walking wounded, continued to carry them in relays until we spotted a stores trolley parked by a building. It was just what we needed. We borrowed it and loaded our stiffs onboard.

Because of the trolley was too narrow to load all three on lengthwise we had to drape them crosswise. Like bunch of dead baddies in the cowboy movies, dangling limp over a saddle.

But one kept coming too; trying to get up so kept rolling off the trolley! So we chucked him on lengthways, on top of, and at right angles, to the other two, and thus stabilised the load. 'Stiffs' is probably the wrong term to describe our mate's condition as they were more like waterlogged oversize rag dolls!

We got a frosty reception when we finally arrived back at the hut from the few who had decided on an early night. But they did help with our 'sleeping beauties' and we got them into their beds. We then collapsed into our own pits and also slept the sleep of the dead.

When I think back on it now, it seems a foolish episode. Our mates, that night had drunk themselves unconscious and it could have had serious consequences. But no harm came to them and we all just suffered almighty hangovers. And one had bruises and black marks on his face, which appeared to be trolley tyre marks? God looks after drunks and fools and we certainly fully qualified on both counts on that occasion.

The following week we moved back to our old hut in 'Y' lines. It smelled of new paint and creosote but didn't seem to look any different. It was still the same drab colour scheme, cream and green everywhere.

Before we moved out of our temporary billet in 'W' lines we had to pay for 'barrack damages'. Damage that we may have caused that was not due to 'fair wear and tear'. We were each charged one shilling and threepence each (7.5p) for a cracked windowpane, a crack we were sure had been already there when we moved in? But we couldn't argue with the corporal who demanded the cash, so we just paid up.

The course was soon in its final week and it was 'panic stations' with the exams and tests looming. The pressure was on and the threats of FT (Further training, being re-coursed) came thick and fast from the training staff. No doubt, some of us would face the "Why for you fail" interview by the OC (Officer Commanding) School. The flight -lieutenant OC was Polish and well known for that opening line when interviewing course failures.

I was confident about the practical operating tests but not so sure about the written tests as so much of the 'theory' seemed so irrelevant to the tasks we performed. But I have already whinged at length about that issue.

Some of the radar theory was interesting but it involved learning formula and equations useful to engineers but had little use to we mere operators. But we were required to use the formula and equations to solve problems in radar theory for the purpose of the tests. However, that knowledge did prove to be useful later, when I got involved in the engineering aspects of radar. But that was to be more than twenty years later!

As already mentioned, we were given very little opportunity to study our notes because of their security classification. We had mock tests and exams. I did well in the practical but was scraping through in the written tests.

In the, so described, written exams, there was, in fact very little writing involved. They were the 'x in the box' optional answer papers. Known as 'vote for Joe' tests, similar to the 'attestation' papers.

The optional answers were confusing. For example, what was the wavelength of particular radar, 1.2, 1.3, 1.5 or 1.7 meters? In practice the radar could be tuned to over most of these wavelengths but only one was the acceptable answer! Also, to avoid mutual interference, no two radars, even though many miles apart, shared the same wavelength.

There were many questions in the papers like that one. Our practical training was excellent, and most of it proved to be relevant, but very little common sense seemed to have been applied to formulating theory training and tests.

We did have a few revision periods with an instructor emphasising particular segments of required knowledge. We took this selected revision as an obvious pointer as to what might come up in the written tests. It had come to us via 'Rumour Control' that this was the system.

'Rumour Control' being a term used in the Service for that mysterious source of all good, but more often bad, news. But such rumours could often turn out to be right, and so 'Rumour Control' was considered to be a reliable source of information. Also, it was nearly always more interesting, than information issued from official sources. But then, speculation is so often more interesting than the final truth!

The test and exam day, or days, came, as the process was spread over several days. I did surprisingly well it the written test. I did very much better than I had done in the mock tests. I was well pleased and very relieved.

The practical tests did not go a well as I expected and there seemed to be a lot more pressure and an impatient attitude shown by our examiners. More so than we had ever met in the mock tests! But the indications were that I was getting through. I earnestly hoped I would pass. Pass now and there was then a good chance of getting home on leave for Christmas, before posting to my first operational unit.

Our final test was in Crew Duties, where we were tested as a radar observing and tracking team. On the test day the course was divided up into crews of three and each crew tested in turn. It quiet late in the afternoon by the time my crew were called for testing.

Our examiner was Sgt Fitton and he was not in a good mood. Testing was getting behind because of equipment failures and trainees not displaying the best of abilities. We were the last crew of the day for testing and we were apprehensive. I was first on the plotting table and all went well with a new plot building. I then changed to observing and I thought that went well too. And so did height operating.

However, when I changed back to plotting, the plot on the table seemed to have little to do with what the observer was reporting? Sgt Fitton started shouting at us but we thought that was part of the act to distract us and put us under pressure. Then the observer reported 'radar tripped' meaning he had lost the display. But this was not part of the exercise; the equipment had really failed again. But it was soon restored and we started the cycle all over again. And we cocked it up all over again!

Sgt Fitton lost his patience with us and banged his fist on the top of the PPI console! The radar screen flared up, then died and plotting ground to a halt! Sgt Fitton then yelled at us, "All right, all right, I've seen enough. Leave it, go!" We went, with the certainty in our minds that we had failed?

I was to serve with Ron Fitton some years later. By then he was a warrant officer and I was a sergeant. I reminded him about that farcical test session and it seemed very funny with those years in between.

But we were not laughing on the day of the test and we were not wrong in thinking that we had failed. Very soon we were told so, our whole crew had failed. But we were not alone as a good many others had too. We were informed, however, that the OC School would make a final decision. We would be interviewed individually the next morning.

That next morning the OC's outer office was very full with those waiting for interview. Soon I was marched in to see the OC. His first remark was as expected, "Why for you fail" but he added, "And you regular too". Meaning that as a volunteer with a career in mind I should, somehow, have done better.

But I had no answer for my failure as I though I was doing well up to the Crew Duties test. But the OC said I had not done to well in DR Navigation. I thought I had made only one error. But a serious error as it happened. It seems that when asked for 'pigeons' I had given a reciprocal bearing. Instead of back to base I would have sent the aircraft off in the opposite direction! The OC decided that I was to have, as he put it, "Two veeks FT". I was then dismissed and marched out of his office and told wait for details of my further training.

In the outer office the flight-sergeant consulted a large wall chart and informed me and the other FTs that we would be joining a new course after Christmas. Not a totally new course but one in its final two weeks. And as I would join that course immediately after Christmas home leave was out of the question. My first Christmas in the RAF was to be spent on a station.

Until I joined the new course I and the other failures were to stay on in the same hut. But soon we would be just that handful as our successful hut-mates left for Christmas leave and posting. Now with just seven of us, the hut suddenly seemed very spacious and quiet. And all but one on the little gang I went around with were now gone too.

But we were not to be left idle while we waited. Until we restarted trade training we would be used as 'fatigue wallahs' doing odd jobs around the station. My first assignment was working in 'Y' lines Airman's Mess, in the plate wash and tin room.

Just two of us were allocated to that task. It was dirty but warm work and we were kept very busy. The plate wash was an experience, having to wash thousands of pieces of crockery after every meal. We started as a three-man team, the third being on the mess staff.

He was an Admin Orderly, someone without a specific trade, and the rank of AC, just like ourselves. Being staff, he decided adopt a superior attitude and tried to order us around. In much the same way as Jimmy, the LAC, at Aldergrove.

But our lad here had naked sleeves just like myself, and my workmate, so we told him told him to wind his neck in. He did, and also found he had jobs to do elsewhere. The two of us laboured on without his assistance.

It was very hard work as we were also responsible for sorting the swill. When used plates came in at the washroom hatch we had to scrape residue food into bins, making sure no other waste other than food went in.

The plates were then placed in special metal trays and passed through a pressure wash and steam-drying machine. At the clean end we had to inspect the plates to ensure they were properly cleaned before stacking them on racks. Any found still with traces of food had to be hand washed. Often plates would come through the washing process still with small green spots. This was dried parsley, which the cooks seemed to use with great abandon. It proved stubborn to remove from the crockery, even with a wire brush. The quick-drying process had baked it on.

This duty started in the morning after breakfast and went on until about 7pm, after the evening meal. But we had to do that job only for a few days and were then rotated onto other tasks in the mess. On finishing our spell in the plate wash the flight-sergeant IC mess came in to see us. She was a member of the WRAF and had a reputation for fierceness.

We thought we must be in trouble. But far from it! She thanked for the work done and having done so well with just two of us. The SAC cook, who supervised us, remarked later, "Blimey, that's a rarity, getting praise from her, all we get is blue shit from Xmas to breakfast!"

It was true she seemed hard on her staff but was still respected and well liked. She was kindness itself to we poor sprogs. When she was not around, or out of earshot, the staff referred to her as 'Bloody Mary'!

I had just one session in the tin room, cleaning all the roasting trays and other metal utensils used in the kitchen. A very messy job having to clean the baked on and blackened residue from what seemed acres of metalwork. It was a job normally reserved for defaulters and staff who had fallen foul of 'Bloody Mary'.

The fatigue parties were normally made up of those who had time to spend either waiting for courses to start or waiting for posting to new units at the end of training. And those like myself who had failed and had to wait to slot into a new course. There was a rumour that failures would often be engineered to generate spare bodies for these odd jobs. I am sure my failure was genuine, but there always seemed to be enough failures and spare bodies to provide the required additional labour.

Defaulters, those doing 'jankers' for minor offences against the rules, also made up the fatigue parties. Again it was rumoured, that finding yourself on a charge could well have been a matter of filling local work quotas? And there was the story that holes in the station perimeter fence were left un-repaired in order to generate defaulters?

On Friday evenings, and at other times, many would exit the camp through holes in the fence instead of the bother of booking out via the Guardroom. In most instances people got away with that, but on some occasions they would not. The RAF police would sometimes wait in ambush to catch the unwary using these unapproved exits! The holes in the fence were never repaired! Thus supporting the rumour that they were purposely left so as to generate spare labour?

The holes in the fence were much favoured and frequently used by many of the NSAs. That route out avoided the queues booking out at the Guardroom and delay in getting out onto the main road for quick start to 'hitching'. But getting caught would result in a weekend spent on camp and on fatigue duties.

For the poorly paid NSAs, hitching lifts was the only way most could travel home at weekends. Most drivers would stop for a uniform in those days so it was a cheap, and sure way to travel, for Servicemen. Scores would be on their way after only short waits for lifts. Often when we went walking in uniform, just for the pleasure of it, vehicles would stop and lifts offered!

General cleaning in the kitchen was just as arduous as the tin room. Having to clean out all those big pots and caldrons was a hard and messy task. One of my jobs was to keep the floor clean. The floors and all surfaces were hosed with hot water several times a day and scrubbed with bass-brooms.

Dirt and food debris would run into channels in the floor and flow down drains. On one occasion while I was swilling the floor a drain became blocked and one of the cooks came to help me to clear it. This he did with the ladle he was using to stir a large caldron of soup. He just scooped out the blockage with the ladle and went straight back to stirring the soup with it! When he saw my questioning look he just grinned and kissed his fingers in the French chef manner and uttered, "Mmaw, added flavour". I decided to take his word for that but gave soup a miss for a few days.

Although the mess used a mountain of potatoes each day we did have to do the peeling? I was glad to discover that a machine performed that task. The bulk of the task, at any rate, but we were still involved in 'spud-bashing'! We had to examine each peeled spud, remove the eyes and any blemishes with the knives of our personal eating-irons.

Dress, while we were on cookhouse fatigues was the ubiquitous green denim boiler suit. In the largest sizes available and already ingrained with dirt and grease. We looked like green and greasy penguins. Underneath we wore our issue blue shirts with detachable collars with tie, but never allowed to remove the tie and collar no matter how hot, steamy and sticky it got! Or how dirty the job got. Still in collar and tie even while working with the pigswill!

Pigswill was a substantial by-product of the mess and it all went to a locally located, nationally known, pork product manufacturer. They bred their own pigs and paid for the swill in pork products, mostly sausages. These sausages were on the menu for most meals so a lot went back into the pigswill. And so were recycled back into sausages again, ad infinitum, by the pigs consuming remnants of their relatives!

Our hobnailed boots, proved a real hazard on the greasy tiled kitchen floor. As mentioned the floors were frequently hosed with hot water but still we has constant slips and falls. Because we were required to carry our mugs, looped on our kitbag cords tied round our waists, a slip meant goodbye to that article. Having to purchase a new mug was guaranteed, by the end of that duty.

At end of the day's kitchen duty our poor boots would be soaking wet and with bleached white patches. Fortunately, because of our early start, we were excused morning working parade so our boots escaped close scrutiny.

~ Chips for Breakfast ~

When the spell on kitchen duties ended I became a general 'gofer' but was mainly employed on the Christmas preparations. That included putting up Christmas decorations in 'Y' lines NAAFI and the Airmen's mess. I cannot properly remember which but I believe it was 'Z' lines Airmen's mess. All junior ranks remaining on the station over the Christmas period used that mess, as 'Y' lines and other messes were closed for the Christmas holiday.

One afternoon when we had gathered back in hut, having finished work early, two SACs came in. They were selling tickets for a raffle. The prize a motorcycle, which they had outside and we could inspect it. Tickets were a shilling each. We took a look at the bike, and old Norton but in good working order. One of us asked why not sell but they said no one would offer the £20 it was worth and the raffle should raise that amount or more. However, they said they would stop selling once they sold £20 worth of tickets and if they did not reach that amount the money raised would become the prize. The odds seemed good so we all bought tickets, all of us at least two to better our chances. But why did I have a funny feeling that I had just given two bob away?

In the meantime we handful in the hut continued with our odd jobs. One of those jobs was to help with the decorations in the Officers mess. Just three of us were detailed for that task. It was an all day job, which entailed moving furniture, including a piano and preparing a room for a function. We were supervised in the task by a flight lieutenant, who seemed to be involved in the management of the Mess. In his forties, he had a pilot's brevet and two rows of medal ribbons. He treated us very well and kept addressing us a 'gentlemen'!

We had not finished by our normal teatime and he asked us if we would work on late to complete the job. We could have our evening meal in the mess. It was a request, and not an order. We agreed as the prospect of a meal in the Officers mess was attractive.

We had that meal, dead on the dot of 5 pm, served in the small staff room off the kitchen. The food was good, as I remember. But nothing special, but tasted the better for small scale cooking. Living in the Officers Mess had that advantage.

We continued working after our meal and had finished our job of putting up some simple and, of course, tasteful Christmas decorations in the mess bar. After we had completed the job our officer went behind the bar and produced four beers, saying, "Sorry, gentlemen, Officers mess, we don't serve pints".

We were very surprised and grateful, but ill at ease. Our officer sensed this and said, "Don't worry, there's only us until twenty-hundred". He then raised his glass and wished us a happy Christmas and thanked us for our efforts. And after a short while of general conversation as we finished our beers we left for our hut, which was only a short distance away.

When we arrived back in the hut there were a few of the others sitting around? One asked why we were so late and how did we manage to miss tea? We told him we had been invited for drinks and dinner in the Officers mess! We got a look that said, "Ask a silly question!"

~ Chapter XIII ~

Christmas Day in 1953 fell on a Friday, but by Wednesday evening the station was almost deserted. Except, of course, for duty staff and the poor sad gits like myself who would or could not get home for the holiday. But we few left in the hut were looking forward to a nice quiet few days without working parades and the scourge of the corporals. A blissful prospect indeed!

On Christmas Eve, all we 'stay behinds' in the hut went into Caln for the evening. But it was closed! Or so it seemed. The pubs in the town that we sometimes frequented were all but deserted. After a very quite half in two of the pubs we decided to head back to camp.

It being Christmas Eve there was a very reduced bus service, so we started walking. On the road back we came to a pub that seemed to have some signs of life so in we went. There was quiet a crowd and many in RAF uniform, some from Yatesbury and others from nearby RAF Compton Basset. Among them was one of my old mates form the Irish Flight who was on the Wireless Operators course there. Also stuck on camp for Christmas.

Over beers we compared notes about our training and its pros and cons. He was not happy learning Morse code as it was monotonous and mind numbing. As he put it, listening to beep, beep, F__ing beep, all day was driving him crackers. Some, he said, had actually gone crackers, or close to it. They had broken down under the pressure of training and had to quit the course! He was not sure that he would make it all the way? I called to mind that Wireless Operator had been my original choice of RAF trade?

But it was Christmas so we put worries and concerns aside and got on with the seasonal merriment. I wish I could remember the name of the pub, as it was a grand old country inn. No great shakes in décor or furnishings but a friendly place with warmth that did not just come from the big roaring open fire.

Carol singing broke out, almost choral in quality, as it seemed that we had more than a few Welsh among us. But the drinking and singing came to an end all too soon as 'time' was called at 10 PM sharp. No extensions in those days, but I suppose the landlord and his staff wanted their Christmas too.

We started our chilly walk back to camp but soon a bus caught us up. We were not at a stop but it did pull up and the conductress called out, "Yatesbury camp". The Yatesbury contingent piled on, jeering and cheering as we left our Compton Basset friends to march home in the cold and dark.

We were all in uniform, greatcoats and boots. As I was scrambling on I stood on the foot of the conductress, causing her to yelp out in pain. I apologised. She was small pretty girl and it was a very small foot, so it must have hurt. I offered to kiss it better but she clouted me with her ticket holder, and retorted, "Cheeky bugger! I should charge you double fare for damage." But it was a friendly wallop and remark, delivered with a smile.

The carol singing continued on the bus but it seemed we had had lost the best voices. They must have been among the Compton Basset crowd. So we journeyed on to the strains of 'Good King Wenceslas', rendered in a manner that must have had the poor old boy spinning in his grave.

The bus soon arrived at the main gate and as we all tumbled off the singing stopped in the realisation that we needed to summon up every ounce of sobriety in order to book back in at the Guardroom. We filed past the window under the baleful gaze of the duty RAF copper. The times and signatures now being entered not quiet as steady handed as those when outbound. The police corporal snapped, "You lot been drinking?" But his scowl quickly turned to a broad grin and he wished us a Happy Christmas.

Clear of the Guardroom the carols started again, every bit as un-tuneful as before and all the way back to the hut. As we reached the hut there was an outbreak of 'shushing' until we remembered we were all together and no one in the hut to disturb!

We sat up chatting until well after midnight with the lights on, forgetting the time and the twenty-three hundred lights out rule.

Cpl Ryder, our IC hut, did not appear to remind us? We eventually turned in and lights were extinguished.

But in the dark, as soon as my head settled on the pillow the bed seemed to rotate and I was soon reroute to the bog! It was the first time I had ever been sick as a result of drinking and it was, and never has been, a pleasant experience?

I woke early on Christmas morning with the expected hang-over, a banging headache and a queasy tum. But a trip to the ablutions down the freezing corridors soon cleared my head. It really was cold! The washing water was just tepid and the heating seemed even lower than ever.

It was about 7 am and all the others were still snoring. I decided I would be better off doing off doing likewise so got back into bed. But as I was dozing off nicely the hut door crashed open and a voice boomed out, "A MERRY CHRISTMAS, ONE AND ALL, HO, HO, HO!"

It was Cpl Ryder, in best blue, and beaming! All now shocked awake and sitting up, he had our full attention! He was carrying a bottle? He repeated the Christmas greeting, "Good morning lads. Happy Christmas" He held up the bottle and said, "A little tradition, NCOs bringing you breakfast in bed on Christmas morning". He then went to each bedside locker and poured a good slug into our mugs. He then raised the bottle in a toast and said, "Sup up lads, Merry Christmas".

I raised my mug in toast but as soon as I put it to my lips and my nose sniffed the contents my stomach set up a protest. Rum, and a good strong brand at that! Not my idea of breakfast, especially the way I was feeling just then! I took a sip and swallowed, expecting the worst? But no, it had a warming and calming affect and a few sips later I felt fine! I had now learned the real meaning and effectiveness of 'hair of the dog'?

Cpl Ryder continued in his hearty manner, "Come on lads, we are all messing together today. Breakfast is waiting?" Breakfast had not been our utmost desire that morning and the very thought sent one of our number scurrying for the ablutions! Cpl Ryder then said,

"Ah well, but what about the rest of you. Be ready in ten minutes, I'll march you there, save you walking!"

We were ready in ten minutes but our much worse off friend decided to stay and continue his calls to Hughie! We didn't march to the mess but just ambled along chatting with Cpl Ryder. When we arrived at the mess there were quite a few in as breakfast had been extended until o-ninehundred that morning. Normally noisy, this breakfast was a fairly hushed affair, in spite of the number there? But most seemed to be just having cereals and I realised that hangovers must have been endemic that particular morning! Cornflakes and cold milk was the dish of choice among our little group too.

Cpl Ryder shared our table and did not spare or seem to share our fragility, in his choice of breakfast! He had gone to the servery and came back with a plate heaped with double everything, eggs, bacon, sausages and beans! He exclaimed with a broad grin, "Well, none of you eating this morning. Pity to waste it!" He ate with relish; enjoying his grease-laden meal and the obvious discomfort he was causing the rest of us as we suddenly went off our cornflakes.

Seeing our sudden lose of appetite, he said, "Good thing. Save yourselves for lunch. Full traditional Christmas dinner. The SNCOs and officers will be serving. Be here, and in number ones". It sounded attractive, but I was not enamoured with the thought of food, however good, at that very moment.

A thought occurred to me? Perhaps the raffle for the motorcycle would be drawn today?

I asked Cpl Ryder if it would take place? At first he looked miffed and then he started laughing, "You fell for that one," he said, shaking his head. It appeared that we had been conned, had fallen for the oldest scam in the book! I had a feeling that it was dodgy but still gormless enough to have paid for tickets! Cpl Ryder, although highly amused by our naivety but said we should report the matter at the Guardroom as soon as possible.

After breakfast, or our morning visit to the mess, as would better describe it, we had a few hours of 'pit bashing' and allowed hangovers to fully subside. I dozed off and when I awoke my stomach was protesting again? But this was a positive and welcome protest! Hunger pangs!

By lunchtime we had all made a full recovery. Even the worst case among us had joined the land of the living and was now looking forward to a meal. We donned our number ones and made for the mess at the appointed hour.

When we arrived we discovered a surprising transformation had taken place since breakfast? The tables were all laid in festive order. There were Christmas crackers, bowels of fruit and nuts, tins of cigarettes and drinking glasses! Around the sides of the dining hall were SNCOs and officers all with beaming smiles. We took our seats in silence, somewhat subdued by this unusual situation.

A squadron-leader announced himself as representing the Station Commander and said 'Grace'. Then we were served with our Christmas meal. It was a full turkey dinner, with all the trimmings, followed by the traditional Christmas pudding. Just before the pudding was served a cook had made a formal entrance bearing a flaming pudding, to cheers and applause.

During the meal, SNCOs and officers were moving among us and keeping our glasses filled with ale. It was very pale ale, a bit on the weak side and more like a shandy. One or two cynics among us suggested that it had been watered down, as they didn't want us to get too pissed and out of hand.

My own little bit of cynicism rendered an opinion the bonhomie from some of the officers seemed a little forced. But it was a Christmas tradition of the Services and everyone was entering into the spirit of the occasion. A hut-mate next to me, the one that had suffered the worst hangover, was less enthused. He muttered something about "patronising bastards"!

As soon as the meal had finished most of our betters left, but some remained and joined in the drinking and general singsong that developed. Most of the SNCOs had stayed on and quiet a few officers. I did notice that most of those remaining and joining in the general fun, wore aircrew brevets and war service medal ribbons?

Except for two young WRAF officers who seemed to be really enjoying it all. All the cooks and kitchen staff also joined in so I spared a thought for the poor fatigue wallahs who would have to deal with the backlog of dishwashing and cleaning. It was late afternoon and getting dark by the time 'lunch' came to an end. One of the senior cooks made an announcement as we were breaking up, "There will be tea this evening in any of you who want it. That's if any of us are sober". But we were too full to even contemplate another meal at that stage. A few hours 'pit bashing' was now what was in mind.

We had that few hours 'pit bashing', also a bit of reading. It was a rare opportunity to read a book now with the hut so unusually quiet. And quiet reigned for several hours until there was a loud yawn from one of our number, who exclaimed, "I'm feeling peckish, anyone fancy going to tea?" "Go on your own, you gutsy git" was the only reply he got!

Also, it was nearly 7 pm so too late for the mess. But off went our hungry friend and was soon back! Someone said, "There, told you so, mess closed!" "Closed F___**", was our mates reply. "Look at this", he went on. He unwrapped a large greaseproof paper parcel containing a heap of turkey meat, including the best part of a huge drumstick and a pile of mince pies "Ah, nice of to think of your mates" I remarked. But he responded, "Bollocks, go get your own. You can just help yourself, the cooks are all pissed".

Driven by greed rather than hunger, the rest of us made for the mess. It was still open and there were a few people in. There was no one serving, and not a cook in sight, but plenty of food on the servery? It was all remnants of the Christmas lunch, now cold or nearly so.

We were not yet really hungry but knew we would be later so like our mate, decided to stock up. We found some greaseproof paper and serviettes and packed a selection from the cold buffet and returned to the hut. We were mindful that we were committing a chargeable offence of removing food from the mess. That was among the more serious 'do not's' that we were subject to. But being Christmas there was no one about to enforce the rules even if they were inclined to do so.

However, we soon destroyed the evidence by scoffing the lot! As we were stuffing ourselves someone remarked that it would have nice to have had something to drink, even some of the weak ale we had earlier. With that remark, another of our mates went to his locker and produced a large 'screw-cap' of beer! There was enough for a good half mug each, which went down nicely. Someone proposed a toast, "Here's to our Courts Martial, so drink up". And so reminding us of our second serious offence of the evening! That of having and/or consuming alcohol in the billet! The rum in the morning was tradition but strong drink at any other time was strictly forbidden. But for today we were free of authority and even Cpl Ryder was nowhere to be seen.

On the Sunday morning, Boxing Day, no one disturbed us. Some of us did go to late breakfast and almost had to do with just cornflakes again! The cooked food had all the hallmarks of a disaster in the kitchen! Burnt scrambled egg, black lace trimmed fried eggs, cast iron bacon and very, very baked beans. The cooks must have been still pissed or suffering from almighty hangovers. The servery was unmanned, so we served ourselves with no risk of overindulging in what was on offer. Finding something edible to put on a plate that was an achievement. We glimpsed one or two of the cooks as we had breakfast and could confirm our opinion that hangovers were indeed the most likely reason for the burnt offerings.

Later in the morning as we were 'pit bashing', Cpl Ryder came in and boomed out, "Nice day, lads, nice flying weather. Who wants to go flying?" We were all attention, of course, but he was grinning in a manner that said some form of joke was involved. He continued, "Anyone know what a Link trainer is?" It seemed we all knew about the Link trainer, it being a basic flying simulator that never left the ground. But a few of us were still interested, so Cpl Ryder said he would arrange for us to have a session on the trainer that afternoon. "We'll see it there any potential pilots among you", was how Cpl Rider put it.

That afternoon, Cpl Ryder and the interested few of us, went to a building that looked like a training centre. Another corporal met us there. He was of Cpl Ryder's vintage, also with lots medal ribbons and an aircrew brevet.

We were taken into a large room that housed the Link trainer and its ancillary equipment. The Link trainer is just a very basic single seat aircraft cockpit simulator, with the basic controls and instruments of a single engine aircraft. It is shaped like a little 'Noddy' aeroplane complete with stubby wings and tail unit. It is mounted on a gimballed platform and responded to the controls in the manner of an actual airborne aircraft.

Associated with the Link trainer was a plotting table with a map under Perspex with an electro-mechanical pen system. This device traced the flight-path as 'flown' by the Link pilot. This whole setup was used to teach basic blind (instrument) flying.

Cpl Ryder explained that today we would have a little flying competition among ourselves. We would each fly a simple 'dog-leg' from points 'A' to 'B' to 'C' marked on the map and see who could best keep to the planned route?

The controls and instruments of Link were explained. But I, like most lads who had grown up through the war years, I had a useful knowledge of an aircraft cockpit layout.

After the brief I was in the cockpit before Cpl Ryder and finished saying, "Who's first".

The blacked out canopy was closed and I 'took off' to fly my little flight plan.

On the first leg I had to climb to an altitude of two thousand feet and be at that height before I reached point 'B'. I turned onto the planned compass heading and started the climb. I enjoyed this schoolboy indulgence for about four minutes then the Link stopped running and the canopy was lifted. It was Cpl Ryder. He said, "You've crashed chum, come and see!"

I climbed out of the Link and went to the table. The pen had traced my four-minute flight, which was just a simple straight line. A grinning Cpl Ryder said, "Look carefully and tell me why you pranged?" I studied the map around the point where my flight had ended and saw the reason right away! The trace had stopped just short of a contour line indicating three thousand feet? It appeared that I had flown into a mountain!

I could also see that I was well off course, wondered why and soon found out why! Because I had been so eager and had jumped into the Link without waiting to be asked, the rest decided to play a little joke by way of teaching me a lesson. Cpl Ryder had put in a simulated wind-speed and direction that would take me into the mountain! And thus, I had also been given a very good practical lesson in DR navigation! A far better lesson than all the hours, so far, spent with the Craig computer.

We played the blind flying game all afternoon and I managed to complete the planned flight a least once! At the end of the session I asked Cpl Ryder if there were any potential pilots among us, to which he replied, "Oh yes, you all have the makings of pilots but you will need bloody good navigators in your crews"

Apart from the Link flying, the rest of the Christmas break was a pretty boring few days. During the day our time was spent just 'pit bashing, reading and attending mediocre meals. Although the cooks were on duty, I think their cooking skills had taken a holiday?

We spent the evenings in the NAAFI watching TV and having a few drinks. The NAAFI bar was less crowded than usual because of the holiday but enough to make it sociable, especially as quiet a few of the WRAF always came in.

The jukebox seemed to the main attraction for them as they played it incessantly all evening long. Top of the charts at that time was Eddy Calvert playing 'Oh Mine Papa' on the trumpet. I must have heard that number played over a hundred times that Christmas. The girls had it on the jukebox about every other tune. I cannot remember other tunes from that time but on the occasions I have since heard that number, it took me right back to RAF Yatesbury and Christmas 1953.

On the Monday following Christmas I, and a few of my hut-mates were put on admin duties sorting out stationary and forms for courses soon to start. We restarted training a couple of days later staying on the same hut but were joined by others from other courses. Although we paraded together each morning we did not all train together and the 'team' identity was now gone. But all sharing the close space of the hut and sharing the same situation imposed on us a group identity. New friendships quickly formed and we soon had new mates joining us in our social activities.

We had a few Scots in our midst who were looking forward to the New Year celebrations, or Hogmanay, as they called it. But New Year's Eve had little special meaning in England then and no special events were planned. The NAAFI and other Clubs would close at the usual time. No use going off camp as the pubs would also chuck out at the usual time and we still had to book in at one minute before midnight!

However, on Thursday 31st of December in the last hours of 1953 we gathered in the NAAFI with our Scots mates, determined to at least see the old year out. And many others, it seems, had the same idea and a great party was soon in full swing.

That evening the jukebox got a rest as the piano and an accordion, accompanying raucous voices provided the music. And like that train journey to Bridgenorth and other gatherings, not the pop tunes of the day but songs of the war years and an earlier generation.

A fight broke out at one point, between two of our WRAF companions, for reasons unknown? But they settled their differences after a bit of screaming and hair pulling and rolling round on the floor among the fag-ends and beer spills. Another girl decided to entertain us with a strip tease but was bundled off by her mates before it got really interesting!

Two of my hut-mates also got close to a serious falling-out. In a common scenario, involving a woman. I have forgotten those hut-mate's names but I will call them Jim and Tim for the sake of this story.

Jim was sitting on a sofa trying to engage the attention of a WRAF sitting beside him. Tim, sitting in a chair close by was also taking an interest in this same young lady. All went well until Jim had to vacate his seat for a pressing need. But while he was away Tim moved in. On his return Jim was not at all pleased and tried to reclaim his place on the sofa. But Tim insisted on claiming 'squatters rights' and would not move. A heated exchange developed and violence was offered. While Jim and Tim were wrapped up in their confrontation our young WRAF decided it was time to circulate and joined other friends at far end of the room.

With the object of their mutual desire and bone of contention removed, Jim and Tim stood down from combat status and both sat down on the sofa now, with room now for the two of them. They exchanged fags, lit up, and behaved as if nothing had occurred!

I got into conversation with a very pleasant LACW (Leading aircraftswoman). Not at all condescending considering her exalted rank, comparatively speaking. Me being a lowly AC2, and a trainee, at that?

We discovered we had a common interest in sailing and all went well until she mentioned that she went sailing most weekends, weather permitting, with her boyfriend. He was an instructor at RAF Locking! But it was still a very pleasant, and well remembered, evening

There were a few lads there that evening that should well remember the big buxom Scots lass? It appeared that she had decided to celebrate Hogmanay by seeing how many trainees she could initiate before the year ended!

We found out about that only the next day when one of our mates revealed he had been among the initiates! We thought he had gone outside to be sick but now we now knew otherwise! "Filthy, lucky bastard" was our response to that revelation!

All the rest of us had from our New Year celebrations were hangovers, and a normal days training to face! We could have sorely done with the holiday that the 1st of January did eventually become.

●

~ Chapter XIV ~

The year 1954 came in cold and soon we had snow and a deep frost. We quickly learned how inadequate our hut heating was. Our morning ablutions were an ordeal, having to wash and shave in cold or barely tepid water! More than once no water at all as pipes froze up and burst! The heating in the hut completely gave up the ghost?

I discovered that when I woke one morning with my breath condensing in the air. Like most that morning I washed and shaved as best I could still wearing my greatcoat. When I tried to pick up my mug to go to breakfast I found it had frozen to the locker top. Some had found that their boots, left under their beds, had frozen to the floor as melted snow from the night before had turned to ice. In spite of the conditions I do not remember feeling very cold. But at age nineteen, I had the warm blood of youth in my veins.

Paraffin stoves were placed in the ablutions to try and prevent a total freeze up, which gave rise to a rumour? That rumour being that in the event of the ablutions going out of action the camp would close, and those who could get home would be sent home until the freeze was over. That rumour resulted in the stoves being sabotaged! But water, just slightly warm, continued to flow.

Our youthfulness also came out in our marches in the snow to and from the AGRRS. Snowballs would whiz up and down the Flight. The corporals would bark at us now and then but even some of them were not past launching the odd snow missile in each other's direction.

We would engage in snow fights during breaks. Better that than wasting time in pointless queuing in the canteen. However, the Flight-Sergeant IC School soon put a stop to our Winter fun. It seemed that couple of snowballs had hit his and the OC School office windows.

As a punishment we had to spend the next twenty minutes doubling round the site roads. Which kept us warm for the most of that afternoon but did not do much for the mood of our corporal instructors who had to run with us. Running in greatcoats and hobnailed boots on icy roads takes a lot of effort. Many slipped and fell during the run and so tripped others and there was the inevitable 'shunt' on the command to halt! Then most went down like skittles!

And that was not the only running we were required to do! Every Wednesday came Sports afternoon, then universal in the RAF. If not taking part in an organised sports activity, football, hockey, etc. we had compulsory PT or cross-country running. Neither of these a popular activity, in the freezing weather.

Out in the open in PT vest and shorts in near zero temperatures was something to be avoided. But hard to avoid because NCOs searched all huts to make sure there were no shirkers. Of course there were those who attempted to dodge but the NCOs knew all the angles and hiding places.

One particularly bleak Wednesday one of our hut-mates decided he was definitely going to stay in the comparative warm of the hut. He had a good book to get on with. He had us lock him into his locker! It was large enough, being more than three feet wide and six feet high with a low set of shelves to one side. These formed a seat with legs accommodated in the full-length wardrobe side. With his book and a torch he would be comfortable for the hour or so of the PT session. There were air-vents so little danger of him suffocating. He had it all planned and tested out beforehand.

He might have gotten away with it had he not tried to smoke? He lit up, but the little air-vents could not cope with that so he nearly smothered! And so he gave his little game away. His coughing and spluttering and the smoke issuing from the vents alerted a corporal on hut patrol. He was put on a charge but got off with an admonishment. The powers that be, it seemed had a sense of humour!

While the snow lasted our first duty each morning was to shovel and brush any new falls from the site roads and paths of the AGRRS and spread salt and sand on any ice patches. And got into trouble for building a snowman when a WRAF officer complained!

Not for wasting time but because persons unknown had transplanted the large icicle we had used for his nose to another part of his anatomy! Such would not raise a comment today but then regarded as lewd and reprehensible.

The cold snap lasted all of my final weeks at Yatesbury and snow was still on the ground as I sat the end of course exams. Although I had passed the written test first time I did even better this second time?

That not surprising since it was exactly the same paper I had sat a few weeks ago! The corporal invigilator, who was also marking the papers, was very impressed with my result!

Although he had been the invigilator at my previous exam he did not seem to remember me or be aware that I had repeated a previous exam paper? I did not enlighten him and left him with his good opinion of me.

I had no conscience about it, seeing that I had passed the paper the first time round. I was more concerned about passing the practical tests, all of which had to be taken again. I was concerned about passing 'Crew Duties' as that could be gamble. Luck was needed to pass with a crew of people who were chosen at random just before the test! I earnestly hoped that that test would be early in the day and that the examiner would not be Sgt Fitton.

It was Sgt Fitton, but this time I did pass 'Crew Duties! And all other tests, and was duly awarded my 'sparks'. The 'sparks' is the identifying badge worn on the right sleeve, by all those belonging to RAF signals trades. It comprises a clenched hand gripping three lightning bolts. I stitched it on my uniform with as much pride as if it was an aircrew brevet.

Although the course was only of six weeks duration, eight weeks in my case, they were hard weeks. But then, the RAF motto is, *Per ardua ad astra*, which can be translated as 'By hard work, reach the stars'. I may not have reached the stars but felt that I had made a fair effort to earn my 'sparks'.

Those of us who had completed trade training, had to move out of the hut in 'Y' lines to a transit hut in 'W' lines. It was the very same hut I had been billeted in while my original hut in 'Y' lines was being renovated. We would be in transit accommodation for a few of days awaiting our postings.

We soon received the posting notices. My first operational unit was to be RAF Langtoft. I had never heard the name before then, as it had not been mentioned in training as a unit forming the UK air defence network.

'Langtoft' sounded German to me and I had a moment of hope that I was being posted to Germany. But no, Langtoft, I soon discovered, is in Lincolnshire, near the small town of Market Deeping and about ten miles north of Peterborough. However, I was to have two weeks leave before reporting there.

On the day of departure from Yatesbury, as we were vacating the transit hut the corporal IC inspected and demanded a small sum of money from each of us for barrack damages. The damage being a cracked windowpane!

It was the very same windowpane that we had been charged for only a few weeks ago? We pointed out that fact and the corporal seemed taken aback. He did not press further for payment and, red-faced, he remarked that he would look into the matter?

I supposed that it was a rare coincidence that the same trainees could be accommodated in the same hut twice during their stay at Yatesbury. So as I made my departure from that hut and RAF Yatesbury I had the feeling that other trainees may be coughing up for that same cracked windowpane?

All that now occupied my mind was the fact that I was going home on leave. Although it was just on ten weeks since I was last on leave, it had seemed an extremely long ten weeks! I was more than ready for another break so very much looking forward to that visit home.

I was going home with a feeling that I had achieved something even though it had taken me an additional two weeks to do so. Nine weeks really, including my week on fatigues, waiting to join a new course. But I had gained my 'sparks' and with them the dizzy heights of the rank of AC1 (Aircraftsman first class)! I was now an AC Plonk instead of an AC Plonk-Plonk! I believed I was now a trained RAF tradesman with a tenuous toe on the bottom rung of the career ladder.

However, the air defence of the United Kingdom would have to wait another couple of weeks before it would benefit from my contribution. With all the training behind me, home now beckoned. All that was in my mind was the prospect of two weeks very welcome leave, and once again, I had nearly £20 in my pocket.

~ END ~

RAF bed pack.

The Cardington Hangars.

The Link Flying Trainer.

RAF Yatesbury – 1950s.

The White Horse at Yatesbury.

Radar Display Console – 1950s.

RAF Telecommunications shoulder flash.

Type 7 'metric' Radar.

Type 14 'centimetric' Radar (and Gloster Meteor).